Kaibeto Memories

A trader's daughter
remembers growing up
on the Navajo Reservation
at Kaibeto Trading Post
in remote northern Arizona
1936-1960

By Elizabeth Anne
Jones Dewveall

Front cover:
Author Elizabeth Anne in native dress near Kaibeto Trading Post,
circa 1939

Library of Congress Control Number—applied for

Copyright © 2023 by Elizabeth Anne Jones Dewveall
Foreword by William R. Jones and Robert V. Jones
Paperback edition: 978-0-89646-103-1

First edition, 2023
Made in the U.S.A.

Published by VistaBooks LLC
637 Blue Ridge Rd
Silverthorne, CO 80498

Cover and interior design by Katherine Lopez:
Legendary Art & Design, LLC
Grand Junction, CO
legendsartist@gmail.com

Images courtesy of Elizabeth Anne Jones Dewveall,
Robin Varnum, SueAnne Donati Suffolk and
Katherine Lopez unless otherwise noted.

Dedicated to
Julia and Ralph Jones
traders at Kaibeto Trading Post
my parents

Elizabeth Anne Jones Dewveall

•••

Ralph Lee Jones born November of 1890;
died November of 1972.

Julia Houck Jones born May of 1900;
died March of 1982.

•••

ILLUSTRATIONS   **PAGE**

MAPS

Kaibeto Trading Post. Here is where Elizabeth Anne spent much of her childhood. The house where she lived, obscured here by trees, was attached to the trading post (shown on the left). An interior doorway passed from the house to the trading area, keeping traders on-call almost constantly. The main entrance to the trading area, flanked by windows on each side, shows in the center of the more prominent building. The structure on the left is the warehouse for storing supplies and traded merchandise such as hides. This picture is a bit unusual in that it was not uncommon to see in the view here not only horses, but wagons and even a pickup. Natives might also linger, socialize, await a family member's lengthy shopping session, or play card games before or after their trading activity, sometimes all day. – *August 1948*

FOREWORD

By Bob Jones and Bill Jones, Elizabeth Anne's cousins

OUR COUSIN ELIZABETH ANNE spent her early years on the Navajo Indian Reservation at Kaibeto Trading Post. She was the daughter of the trader there. Her trader-father, Ralph Jones, and her mother, Julia, operated this supplier of white-man's goods to local Indians at a time when there was no other source for supplies in that barren land. Bluffs, mesas, and sandy desert were the landscape around this place, then among the most isolated in the United states with something like seventy-five miles including many rut roads to the nearest railroad track. For the Natives, producing a living on this land required ingenuity and perseverance, and the trading post provided some of what was needed to make life a bit easier.

Elizabeth Anne's time at the post was from her birth in 1936 until the early 1960s. Her playmates were often Native children. When Elizabeth Anne reached school age she lived during school sessions in Winslow with her Aunt Zada, Uncle John, and their two daughters so she could attend schools there. But during school breaks and summer vacations when at the trading post, she, too, became a trader, helping with sales and operation of the post. She thus had a youth that was unusual for a girl in America and which led to experiences involving interactions among two cultures.

Several of us in the family have prodded Elizabeth Anne to "write a book" about her Kaibeto Trading Post experiences, but only recently during COVID downtime did she begin to jot down her memories as they came to her day by day. She posted notes on Facebook as she produced one little story after another to share with friends and family and to record the contribution her parents made to the trading post's history. Finally, Elizabeth Anne has agreed to allow her Kaibeto Trading Post memories to be gathered into a book, and many of us are grateful.

Though Elizabeth Anne's wider family includes writers of various kinds, many of us feel she is the best writer among us. Her prose is direct, clear, and has a nice bounce to it. One feels immediately present in her scenes, and her sentences often seem to have a smile on their faces. Sometimes she brings forth a genuine belly laugh without even trying.

Now others can enjoy our cousin's lively, down-home accounts of childhood and teenage years in that remote spot in northern Arizona. The tales, in fact, include a time when Elizabeth Anne and her husband Bob managed Kaibeto Trading Post just as her mother and father did when she was a young-girl there. It's hard to imagine anyone now alive who knows more of the Kaibeto Trading Post operation than Elizabeth Anne does.

In, with, and under some of Elizabeth Anne's memories, we have specific, firsthand instances of respect, friendship, and even deep caring between the trader's family and their customers. And occasionally there is a hint of resentment toward white culture when it seemed not to value Navajo ways. So, along with her delightful telling about her life "on the Rez" as she calls it, Elizabeth Anne has given historians and cultural anthropologists a primary source of information and insight into the ongoing interactions between whites and native peoples in America.

Our cousin wants us to keep in mind that her stories do not portray Navajo ways today. She suspects they now use credit cards or smart phones to pay for things, and she knows many in the younger generation who have been to fine schools and gone on to college and the professions. "The old ways," she says, "are mostly gone."

Readers also do well to be aware that Elizabeth Anne's memories do not proceed in chronological order from her earliest days onward but are set down as she remembers them during those recent weeks of intense COVID concern. Toward the end, she gives dates for the day the memory was written down. As she remembers we are reminded that the memories came interspersed with her daily activities many years later. With but few minor changes, we have remained faithful to what Elizabeth Anne wrote.

When we were in our early teens, the two of us cousins had a great adventure living with Ralph, Julia, and Elizabeth Anne at the Kaibeto Trading Post for a week or so. We rode Indian ponies, watched weavers at work, saw the dog get struck by a rattlesnake (the dog lived), pumped gas, and went trembling into the dark cave to bring in a fresh supply of "total chosie," which is what we thought Navajos called soda pop. So it is our special pleasure to help make a book out of our cousin's captivating stories from her early life. We hope you, too, will enjoy them, learn from them, and gain a deeper appreciation for the life Elizabeth Anne and her parents lived out there in Kaibito. May we also come to understand something of the Navajo culture and the people who have lived it in their wide, barren, and beautiful land.

– *Bob Jones and Bill Jones* (or Bobby and Billy as we were called when we stayed at Kaibeto Trading Post a long time ago)

Elizabeth Anne holding Daddy's hand, while Ralph is in his typical "trader's uniform" for being merchant, warehouseman, mechanic, and more. – *circa 1943*

Elizabeth Anne and Mother Julia in "trader's uniform" for trading in the store. – *circa 1943*

KAIBITO/KAIBETO

NAVAJO WORDS LIKE KAIBITO were initially not written. This may explain why different spellings got attached to different places. Not far from the trading post is a spring that has long been called Kaibito Spring and which may explain why the post was built where it was. Such springs in this region are not unlikely to have willows. From the web page of the K' Ai' Bii' To' chapter of the Navajo Nation we learn that the word "Kaibito" or "Kaibeto" derives from the old Navajo phrase that is expressed in writing as K' Ai' Bii'To'. The web site also tells us this can be translated "willow in the water."

In today's world two spellings of Kaibito/Kaibeto are used for different features: The trading post from far back in time has been spelled Kaibeto as is the Kaibeto Indian School, but the creek that occasionally runs past these places is shown on government maps as Kaibito, as is Kaibito Spring, Kaibito Plateau, and the town of Kaibito but which today has the Kaibeto post office. In Kaibeto Memories Elizabeth Anne always uses her preferred form Kaibeto; elsewhere the separate spellings that have traditionally been applied to separate features have been used. Generally, however, such strict practice is not followed.

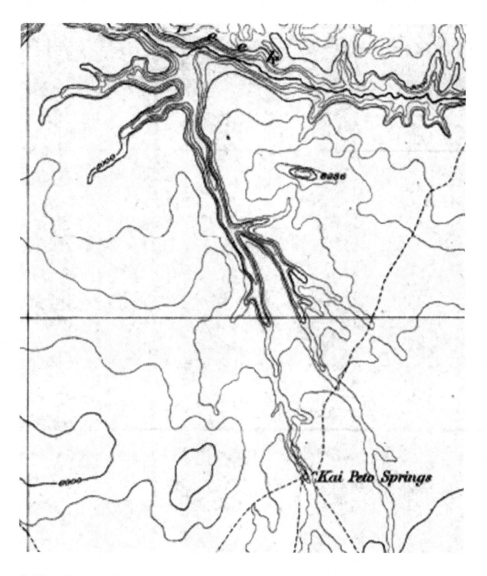

Kai Peto Springs shows on an 1886 map of the Kaibito region. (Editions of this map did not change Kai Peto Springs to Kaibito Springs until 1929, the name that appears on maps today.) Except for scarce springs in otherwise vast waterless areas, there are few place names on even the larger map this one is part of. That may be why four trails with two nearby junctions are shown to converge on this water source. The map shows a trickle of water flowing northward toward the spot where Kaibeto Trading Post was founded circa 1914. Although automobiles began appearing in the area as early as 1920, it was decades before existing tracks became real roads, a process slowly continuing during most of the time that Elizabeth Anne was growing up. Map by U.S. Geological Survey.

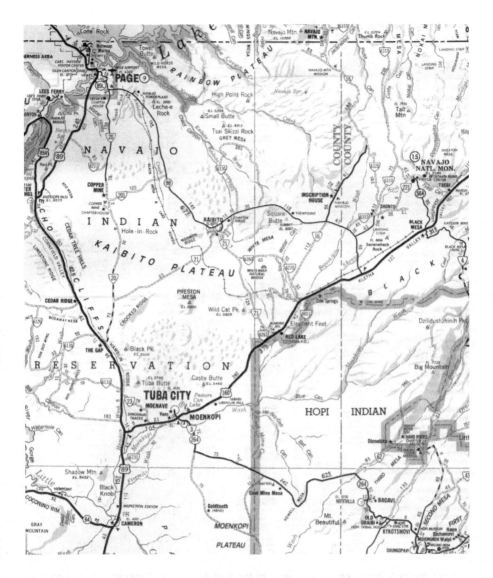

Map of Kaibito region, from Arizona Guide, 2010, courtesy Arizona Office of Tourism.

Kaibeto Memories

A trader's daughter remembers growing up
on the Navajo Reservation at Kaibeto Trading Post
in remote northern Arizona
1936-1960

By Elizabeth Anne Jones Dewveall

[**Editor's Note:** Each memory Elizabeth Anne recorded during her COVID down-time is separated by a space from the next. They are presented in the sequence she remembered them but not necessarily in the sequence in which the events occurred. Her narrative is as she is reporting to Facebook friends, copied here in that form as first-person recorded history.]

And so the story begins...

Catching up on newspaper reading today and feeling sad about the plight of the Navajo people during this pandemic. When my parents were traders on the Rez all those years ago, most Navajo families hauled their water, making it an extremely precious commodity. For about thirty percent of the population this is still true today. A fifty-gallon barrel of water for a week's supply does not make for the recommended frequent hand washing.

People tell me I should write a book about the more than twenty-five years my folks manned that desolate, but beautiful trading post. When you arrived at Kaibeto, you had to leave by the same road you came, for it was truly the end of the line. We had few visitors and those we didn't know, especially if they were Anglo, were looked at with suspicion. During those days, more than one trading post went up in flames along with their proprietors. It was never, ever a Navajo who caused such harm. So, yes, I do have enough trading post yarns to outlast this pandemic and tomorrow I will attempt to bring you one featuring my inimitable father. For today I would ask for your prayers for these dear people who were so good to our family for so many years.

It's one of those days with a multitude of interruptions, so the story I promised yesterday will be tomorrow's tale. Never fear, I have just finished listening to the latest political hoopla surrounding our current situation and it reminded me of a bit of political collusion on the reservation more than a half century ago. After the Suffragettes finished their worthy work, there was still one group in our nation who were denied the privilege of voting. This travesty was eventually corrected, and Native Americans were allowed to go to the polls. Like the rest of us, these tribal citizens first had to register to vote. And in order to register there had to be a registrar. Each trading post had a suitable candidate in the local trader. Thus, my father was duly sworn and left to figure out on his own how to properly process this important steppingstone among a people whose only ID might be a thumb print.

My dad was as honest as any man who ever lived, but he was also a card carrying, straight ticket, die hard Democrat. After explaining the importance of selecting a president and other dignitaries with his rather limited Navajo vocabulary, he failed to find the right words to explain the little box on the registration form which indicated party preference. Needless to say, from that day forward, every Navajo voter in nearly fifteen square miles became a member of the Democratic Party. As terrible as that sounds, it really did nothing to spoil the good old USA ideal of all men being equal. The trader at Tonalea, located about twenty miles to the south was as staunch a Republican as Daddy was a Democrat and he also suffered a loss of his Navajo vocabulary when it came to checking the Political Party box.

Today's trader adventure is a bit indelicate, so if you are the blushing type, just skip on over to the lady who is giving instructions on how to fashion a face mask out of old brassieres. The old-time trading posts were three walled affairs with an area in the center called the "bull pen." This pen was surrounded by a counter with a railing over it so the customer was obliged to stand at a distance from any desired purchase. Shopping was done one item at a time with the shopper pointing to what was needed and the trader then putting that item on the counter. This could be, and often was, an all-day process.

Trading posts sold everything from canned peaches to horseshoe nails so every inch of space behind the counter was precious and shelves were stocked from ceiling to floor. Daddy always stocked the shelves next to the ceiling with unbreakable goods such as boxes of oatmeal or cornmeal. He became very adroit at flicking those down by sliding a broom handle behind them and catching them inches from the floor. This was big entertainment for our customers and always brought an appreciative response. Thus encouraged, Daddy constantly improved his performance, sometimes making a half turn before making his catch at the last possible microsecond.

Sheep were a mainstay in the region's economy. Here an Indian mother is joining in herding sheep while mounted on a pony with a baby in a cradleboard that rests on the saddlehorn. The photographer is unknown, but the Jones family Buick coupe indicates Elizabeth Anne's trader father Ralph was there, where there was a scale and a corral, as the herder was selecting the sheep he wanted to sell. *– Sept 27, 1949*

Then (you can start blushing now) came the advent of women's personal products. Mother had a hard time convincing Daddy that those blue boxes should be included in the inventory, but he finally ordered just one case. Since these were not breakable, they joined the oatmeal and cornmeal on the topmost shelves. And there they stayed and stayed and stayed some more until Daddy could not resist telling Mother that he was right and should not have listened to her about ordering such things. Mother informed him that of course they were not going to sell because everything that came off those top shelves was accompanied by a performance second only to Vaudeville and no shy Navajo lady was going to risk such embarrassment. She recommended moving them to a quiet eye level corner where they could be bought with no fanfare. This meant displacing some canned milk and other important big sellers and was done very grudgingly. Still the pretty blue boxes gathered dust unless Mother or I happened to be in the store. Finally, Daddy realized that no Navajo lady was going to buy such things from a man. So if Mrs. Nez had obviously finished her shopping but remained standing quietly by her purchases, he would bound up the little steps to our living quarters and holler for Mother or me to get down in the store because he was quite sure Mrs. Nez had one more purchase to make. This was always fun for me because as I was making sure the blue box was modestly contained in a plain brown paper bag, the recipient and I would always giggle together as if we were the only ladies in the universe who were privy to such secret things.

I have to confess I nearly wrote this one in my nightie. One little chore led to another and first thing I knew I was sans shower and no earrings and it was noon! I could feel both my mother and my Aunt Zada peering over my shoulder. But on to a very little-known aspect of Navajo trading. In those early days many of the Navajos were herders in every sense of the word. Their flocks of sheep and goats and sometimes even a few cattle were immense, and their lives depended on them.

In spring we bought their wool and in the fall they sold us lambs. If a lamb or goat was slaughtered for personal use, every inch of the animal was put to good use. Even so, occasionally one of our customers would come bearing a sheep or goat skin or even a cow hide. I don't know if Daddy paid fifty cents or five dollars for such because it was not a part of the enterprise I wanted to know about. Daddy stacked these offerings in a far and gloomy corner of our huge warehouse and covered them loosely with a tarp. Getting anywhere near that corner was not a treat for the senses!

Enter Mr. H H Baker who lived in Winslow and who just happened to be my Sunday School teacher when I took my turn at being schooled there. Mr. Baker was employed by Babbitt Brothers (who more or less ran all that part of Northern Arizona in those days) to do such important tasks as getting those animal hides out of trader's warehouses and on their stinky way to become purses or belts. Not only was he a conscientious judge of hides, Mr. Baker (along with his wife) was convinced that the soul of every child entrusted to his teaching was his Godly responsibility and might end up in eternal trouble if he neglected them in any way. Thus, when I was home on the reservation for the summer, Mr. Baker's visit always involved a review of several missed Sunday School lessons. Mr. Baker always had several posts to visit during whatever day he showed up, so due to time constraints, he had to multitask. I was told to sit on a bale of hay while he sorted the sheep skins from the goat skins, the stench and aroma of untanned pelts growing ever thicker while Jesus walked on water or Jericho came tumbling down. When he was finished, Mother always had a nice lunch waiting for him which he ate with great appreciation while I wondered if I would ever be hungry again.

Not many folks can say their earliest memory was formed by stepping on a rattlesnake, but that early childhood scenario has been frozen in my brain for more than eighty years. My grandparents were visiting, and that morning my grandmother had firmly planted my white high-topped lace up shoes upon my feet before I took my first step. Back then, everyone believed that toddlers had weak ankles and that sort of shoe was the answer to the problem.

So be it summer or winter, we all had to wear them, brown for boys, white for girls and ugly as sin. Even so, my detested pair may well have saved my life.

I had just escaped the heat of the kitchen and was walking down a little hill close to the back door, when I felt something squishy under my well shod feet and looked down to discover I was standing atop a big pile of something that reminded me of scales on a fish. I was old enough to know that where there were fish there should be water, so I rushed inside to announce the unusual phenomenon of a fish in our arid back yard. All four adults quickly abandoned the breakfast table as I headed out the door ahead of them to point out my find. They were greeted by the ominous bone chilling buzz only a king size rattler can produce.

My step grandfather, a very genteel jeweler and watch maker, quickly pulled up one very well pressed pant leg in preparation for crushing the snake's head with the heel of his shoe. My father, seeing the danger and impossibility of this move, gave Daddy Self a shove that propelled him all the way to the clothesline pole. With his other hand Daddy grabbed the hoe, kept by the back door for just this sort of occasion, and separated the snake from its head. My mother and grandmother provided appropriate female acoustics while I, thinking that somehow all this violence was my fault, sought shelter behind a nearby washtub.

I don't recall anything else about that day, but it is interesting to note that many years later when my husband Bob and I were running the trading post, our older daughter, seeking to escape nap time, stepped bare footed on a huge bull snake which was sunning himself on the porch step. She also ran to tell me there was a big fish out there. Why three-year-olds equate snakes with fish is beyond me, but at this particular spot in history, we have plenty of time to ponder the answer to that question.

In yesterday's posting I mentioned something called a clothesline pole. It has occurred to me that there may be a few of you out there who have no idea what that might be. Back in the "good ole days" before the advent of General Electric or Whirlpool, God did the clothes drying. This required a long heavy wire strung between two stationary poles. Clothes were pinned on this wire by clever little gadgets called, of all things--clothes pins. If the line was long enough and the laundry large enough, first thing you knew that wire stretched, and your newly scrubbed skivvies were dragging in the dirt. Thus, the clothesline pole which had a ring screwed in its top and could be moved at will to prop up the line and prevent such disasters.

My mother had enough Native American genes to be able to assimilate quite well into the surrounding culture, but she did strictly adhere to the old adage about "washing on Monday, ironing on Tuesday, mending on Wednesday," etc. I am sure there were some ladies in her generation who would have said that mantra could be found in the Bible right along with "money is the root of all evil." There are a lot of things about progress of which we can be critical, but I am thankful I can throw a load of clothes into an electric dryer on a Saturday and not feel guilty. But for today, just for today, we are going to honor my mother's convictions and leave those sheets and towels and Daddy's long johns flapping in the breeze while I find time to send a note or two to some Winslow friends I am sure are risking it all for their fellow tribe members [as they help those stricken by the virus].

My parents were not church attenders as there were no churches to attend any closer than fifty miles away at Tuba City. That may not sound like a formidable distance to us today, but each of those fifty miles was a bone jarring, axle breaking challenge on a road which could change its route daily depending on the last sandstorm. Until the early 50s most trading posts were open from sunrise to sunset seven days per week. When they did begin closing on Sunday, that day was a welcome respite to catch up the multitude of chores involved in maintaining a trading post. Thus, my mother who had absolutely no talent as far as reading future events became a pioneer in our new phenomenon of reaching people online to further their spiritual growth.

We had a radio of sorts (that radio will probably be another story). Every weekday morning at nine o'clock Mother popped up out of the store or dishpan or whatever was claiming her attention and glued her ear to the little radio where a fellow named Al Salter (if I remember correctly) held forth on his "Hour of Power." This was strictly her time with the Lord and no interruptions were permitted. Unless I was home to give Daddy a hand, Hosteen Littleman's horse had to wait for its hay breakfast and John Manygoats's pickup had to park patiently by our lone gas pump. No one ever seemed to mind, and I can't help but think that time she spent might have been one of the reasons our post, although one of the most desolate, was spared all of the catastrophes experienced by so many others.

This is the way we wash our clothes, wash our clothes, wash our clothes, early Monday morning. This is the way we iron our clothes, iron our clothes, iron our clothes, early Tuesday morning. A few of you might be old enough to remember that little ditty. Even though it sounds frivolous, when I was a child, it was a serious reminder of how housekeeping duties were supposed to be conducted.

I have a very vague memory of Mother using a set of irons which were heated on the wood stove, then clamped onto a handle until they cooled and had to be replaced. I think Mother called them "sad irons" but that may not be accurate. What I do have is a clear memory of, and perhaps a scar or two from her next iron. I believe it was made by Coleman (the lantern people) and was equipped with its own little gas tank which was attached to the back of the iron. A tiny pump was used to build up pressure until one could ignite the innards which burned brightly just like the gas grills of today.

There were only a few minor problems. Since the heating unit was mid-section of the iron, the tip remained cool. If you pumped the pressure up high enough to heat the entire iron and tackled the wrinkles on a collar, the rest of your shirt usually became decorated with an iron shaped scorch mark. But this was nothing compared to what happened if you let your arm relax for even a second. Almost as soon as the iron was lit, the small rear gas tank became about the same temperature as the bottom of the iron. Ironing day always involved a few blisters and a definite change in my mother's usual upbeat personality. Daddy and I pretty much stayed in the trading post every Tuesday.

LYSOL! That really was what I was going to write about today and now there is all this hubbub over it [concerning harmful chemicals]. Forget all that. Lysol is another of those products which was around during our trading days and did play a rather prominent part. With all the emphasis on sanitizing in our present state, you may not be ready for this one, but here goes. Every trading post had a drinking bucket sitting on the closest counter to the entrance. Most people traveled long, dusty miles to get there and were very thirsty when they arrived. This big galvanized bucket was filled with fresh water each morning and maybe several times during the day. In the interests of sanitation there was a large dipper inside the bucket. Instead of dipping the provided tin cup into the clean water, the user poured it into the cup which was then used by everyone.

Tuberculosis was rampant on the Rez in those days and my mother had every reason to fear it. She had experienced the disease and was one of those folks who were sent "out west" to prolong her life by maybe a few months. (She stretched that out by over fifty years.) She recognized the danger of this mode of refreshment and did her best to combat it. Her weapon of choice?

Lysol, of course. Back then there was only one Lysol product which came in a little brown bottle and poured out in a thick goo which instantly turned white when added to water. Every night our bucket got a thorough scrubbing with a Lysol solution ten times stronger than recommended and the poor little tin cup was completely submerged until the next day dawned. The surrounding counter was also thoroughly swabbed and left dripping. Mother would have dismissed the wipes we use today as not worthy of notice. Daddy and I both hated the noxious odor of that solution but our complaints were ignored. That area always smelled faintly of Lysol and although I know she rinsed the bucket and cup thoroughly every morning, I am also certain the water at our trading post had a slightly different taste than at some of the others.

A bit of a change today for some blessing counting. Yesterday we had a visit (we kept all the covid rules) from our younger daughter and her husband. They brought our dinner and as we "mimed" our parting hugs, I couldn't help but think of the first hug this child ever had nearly sixty years ago.

Carole was our "trading post" baby and a third addition to our family. Elaborate plans were made for her safe arrival, and a cabin was rented where my parents would stay with our other girl and boy as the delivery time grew near. The local medicine man kept telling me we were going to way too much trouble because he could take care of me just fine. In retrospect, we probably should have listened.

The big day arrived, and Daddy drove me to the hospital, and calmly stayed with me through labor. He was the one who realized it was time for me to finish up the job we had begun and alerted the nursing staff. Then, in a few short moments, due to the incompetence of the doctor and staff, we came very close to having a still born baby. (Something about a coffee break?). It took a lot to get my dad riled up, but when he realized that I had been left alone in the delivery room, the most skilled matador in Mexico would have been shaking in his cape if he had to confront Daddy.

When the crisis was over, the doctor handed the baby in all her newborn ickiness to my father and told everyone if that old man didn't know that she was okay they were likely to have him as a patient. I think his real reason was that he knew that with his arms full of newborn baby, my father would not be able to chase him down and strangle him. Carole got her first embrace from the grandfather she came to adore. God looked after us that day and continues to do so through all three of our precious children. I am so thankful.

Looking at our car gathering dust in the carport this morning made me think of my dad's old maroon Buick which never lacked a nice protective coating of Arizona dust and sometimes sported several layers of mud/clay on each fender. It was either a 1940 or '41 two door affair with a tiny back seat. He acquired it shortly before WWII broke out, so he was stuck with it for the duration. During its ten-year life span it served us well even though when traded in it was more baling wire than Buick.

Its most important feature was a massive trunk which was sacred ground and never to be meddled with by wife or daughter. Along with all the jack handles and other paraphernalia which always comes with cars, it held other equally important items. Stuffed into one corner were at least a dozen gunny sacks. Alongside those was another gunny sack which was filled with several cans of Vienna sausages, tins of sardines, boxes of saltine crackers, a big box of matches, small pieces of kindling tied together, rolled up newspaper, a roll of toilet paper, and a wicked looking pocketknife. Several blankets hid a set of chains in another corner. Atop all this was a medium size axe and full-size shovel. Most important, there was a huge canteen of water which was always full.

Thanks to the gunny sacks which provided great traction when thrown under a mired wheel, after one applied the jack, I never got to experience a delicious repast of crackers and sardines while being stuck in sand or mud overnight. There were a couple of times that it took Daddy so long to extract us from whatever predicament we were in that I did get to drink from the canteen. Alas, he wasn't all that particular about changing the water!

The spring I graduated eighth grade, my father came to fetch me driving a black Buick Roadmaster. On the way home he proudly announced that his new acquisition came equipped with something called Dynaflow, so I should easily learn to drive it. A typical Jr High graduate, I was feeling quite grown up, but never dreamed Daddy meant any time that summer. Next morning, amidst her loud protests of "Ralph, she is too young", Daddy left Mother minding the store and we were off for our first driving lesson.

Kaibeto had an airport (that is another story), which was overgrown with tumble weeds but still reasonably flat. It really was easy to stop and start and steer on that clay packed surface (no shifting involved with Dynaflow) so very quickly Daddy directed me to the main road where I was taught the intricacies of reservation driving. Important rules like find a wide spot and pull over when you saw a cloud of dust moving toward you as that meant another vehicle was approaching and would need to pass. Always slow nearly to a stop and hold your breath when you had climbed the hill to the "divide" because the road was rocky there and so no way to know if a vehicle was coming at you head on. And NEVER, NEVER slow down if you see a sand dune up ahead.

When we returned to the trading post, Daddy handed me the keys and informed me that from now on it was my responsibility to pick up the mail. The nearest post office was twenty-four challenging miles away over that same "practice road" and every Monday and Friday were mail days. Mother was still muttering protests as she accompanied me on my first run. She never went along again. I don't know if that was out of fear for her life or because she realized there really was little danger for me.

By the time I turned sixteen many Navajos had reason to drive on state highways so it was decided they should have a license like everyone else. The examiner showed up one morning and now I really was old enough to drive, so I eagerly awaited my turn to be tested. My heart sank when I looked out the window and saw that this test fellow was putting up traffic cones and having all the applicants drive backwards around them and also was requiring them to parallel park. Daddy and experience had taught me many things about driving by then, but we had completely neglected the little R on the gear shift display. With sinking heart, I went to start the black monster, but the only response was that little "click, click" which comes when the battery is kaput. Hot and tired and looking longingly at the road out of our little valley, the man asked me how long I had been driving. I told the truth, and he handed me my license as he told me he figured since I was still alive, I probably would also survive out where there were real roads. To this day I still can't back a car more than a few feet.

I think I was about four years old when I became the "total chosie" (that is what the Navajo word for soda pop sounded like to me) girl at the trading post. Due to coming-of-age rites or the very important curing ceremonies, there were times when a great many extra Navajos gathered in our vicinity. Our "bull pen" would become so packed that Mother had no choice but to join Daddy in waiting on the crowd.

Alas, I was too young to be left to my own devices in the living quarters. The solution to this dilemma was probably against the law, but I think quite ingenious. Our cash drawer was built into the lowest of the many shelves at the front of the store. Soda pop cost a dime, so mother eliminated the penny place, pushed all the other coins down one place and taught me that if someone paid me with a fifty-cent piece then I was to put that fifty-cent piece in its place and for change give them back the coins from those remaining in the row. That would be a quarter, a dime and a nickel. If

Elizabeth Anne and her Kaibeto playmates.

someone paid in pennies, I was told to just throw them in the bottom of the drawer. I had a little stool to climb on and Daddy installed a bottle opener down on my level. About all I had to remember were the words for black (Coke), orange (Nesbitt's), or red (strawberry) and of course that a dime required no change. Everyone soon learned that paying for pop with anything but coin caused a delay while a grown-up was found to make change.

Navajos of that day trained their children to watch sheep when they were at a tender age, so no one even thought to turn my parents in for any sort of child abuse. I thought it was great fun. I didn't learn much, as many years later when I was managing a convenience store, I allowed my fifteen-year-old son to help out in the pop cooler. I caught the dickens from my boss and Lee had to be banished immediately. That worked out okay as the minute he turned sixteen he started working in the grocery business and remains there today. My parents would be quite proud.

Kaibeto Trading Post was built smack dab into the side of a mesa. So I am guessing that the cave carved into that mesa was the beginning of its construction. The door to that cavern loomed as an ominous dark hole situated at the far end of our huge warehouse. I am quite sure, like the walls, the floor was dirt. I never lingered long enough to find out. The cave's temperature remained the same all year and it was used for storing all the "total chosie" we talked about yesterday, plus huge bags of apples, onions, and potatoes.

My father had read me every fairy tale ever written. Thus I was sure that cave was inhabited by all sorts of creatures which not only went "trip, trap, trip, trap" as they followed you to your doom but also shouted, "fee, fie, fo, fum" while they sharpened their knives in preparation to cutting you into bite sized pieces. After all, they had to be somewhere, and the cave would be an ideal habitat. When I grew strong enough to lift a case of pop, Daddy would send me to the cave to fetch it. I never let him know how terrified I was, and I never saw so much as an errant spider in the place.

It was Daddy who showed up for breakfast one morning looking a bit pale and unnerved. He had made his routine supply trip into the cave, sans flashlight, as usual, and came eye to eye with a huge snake. This was a very friendly reptile who just happened to be hanging from some protrusion in the roof. Happy for the company, the snake dropped down around Daddy's shoulders, giving him a big hug as he slithered off into warehouse. 'Twas only a bull snake, but I never saw Daddy go in the cave again without flashlight in hand.

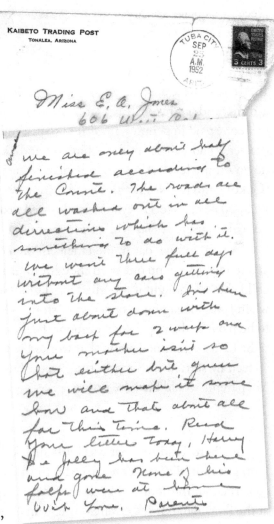

One of my daughter's friends asked me today if Kaibeto still existed. Sadly, it has gone the way of at least ninety percent of the old-time trading posts. Last time we were in the area, there was nothing left but a

Letter to Elizabeth Anne at school on road conditions on the way to the Kaibeto Trading Post. - *1952*

good portion of the pump house and a few walls from the old government school. The trading post had been so decimated that I had a hard time figuring out what went where. I like to think that the huge tin roof, the thousands of stones, and the Arbuckle coffee box windowsills had all been carted off to make many hogans or sheep camps more livable. There is, however, still a place called Kaibeto Trading Post and it is built in an area we called "up the hill" where the ground is level and there are no sand dunes to slog over or washes to carry you away.

The original Kaibeto was built very close to where two washes converged. I guess the proper word is arroyo, but we called them "Little Wash" and "Big Wash". Big wash can be found on some old maps and shows that it drained a very large area northwest of Kaibeto. Little wash had no such map distinction, but if you walked along it for a couple of miles you were treated to some of the most amazing rock cathedrals and slot canyons God ever created. The only problem with this arrangement was that when it stormed, Kaibeto became more or less an island. It didn't have to rain at Kaibeto itself to make those washes produce bountifully. We knew that when the sky was dark to the north it was very likely we would soon be hearing the crashing and pounding of seething muddy water pushing huge boulders and even trees ahead of it. Very rarely did both washes perform together, but when they did, we always wondered if this would be the time our gasoline tank would get pulled out of the ground. It never was.

The last bit of what passed for a road to the trading post was right across the washes. After every storm Daddy had to round up a crew, hand out the shovels (and the "total chosie") and rebuild. It was not an easy job and sometimes took a couple of days. We still had customers, but they didn't buy as much when it had to be carried across the slimy wash bottom to a pickup parked a quarter of a mile away. I suspect that the last time Kaibeto changed hands, the current trader decided it would be much more sensible to move the whole operation up the hill. That certainly would have been a very wise business decision, but it cost him a life in one of the most beautiful little valleys any of you can imagine.

[In this darn pandemic], it has been some time since we have discussed our various wardrobes as we stay in our abodes, knowing we won't be viewed by anyone but close family. Yesterday I donned my usual garb of a pair of knit pants and a rather nondescript top. My husband promptly declared that he didn't realize I had a doctor's appointment. When I asked him why he thought I was going somewhere, he replied. "You got dressed this morning."

For the past week I have been trying out several floor length lounge dresses which have hung in my closet since before the advent of our oldest great grand. (She is 22). Even though properly accessorized with earrings, my husband must have thought they were night gowns. Today I am making sure he knows which end of me is up by wearing one of my favorites, the mauve one which proclaims, "At my Age I Need Glasses" and features some fancy long stemmed goblets bearing assortments of exotic fruits. I just love the color!

There are many pictures of me during my preschool phase dressed in typical Navajo garb. At age three I was featured on the back cover of Standard Oil Magazine dressed like every little Navajo girl. Posing by our lone gasoline dispenser, I also was sporting a ton of wonderful turquoise jewelry Daddy must have borrowed from the pawn cupboard. [See illustration on page 43.] Truth be told, I often wore overalls, and that was not considered proper for little girls in those days.

Mother must have strayed into the men and boys section of "Monkey Wards" for my clothes, but she must have kept those articles at home, for none of my aunties or my grandmother appear in pictures with me unless I was properly clad in a dress. I was in Junior High when my Winslow mom (Aunt Zada) allowed me to own one pair of slacks--in case we decided to go on a picnic. She also purchased just one pair for herself in order to be modest for bicycle riding. No one ever knew about the pair of men's Levi's awaiting my arrival at home from school every summer. Stiff as boards, it took about two weeks of constant wear to break them in, but after that they were perfect for every occasion.

I don't remember this story at all, but my mother retold it frequently, so it must be true. For many years our trading post was owned by the Richardson family. The Richardsons were a downright dynasty when it came to owning trading posts. Many of you have probably visited the crown jewel of their efforts, a place called Cameron located on Highway 89 about forty miles north of Flagstaff. So it was natural that we stopped at Cameron frequently, for both business and pleasure. The Richardsons knew how to throw a good party, especially at Christmas. This was during the Shirley Temple era when the parents of every daughter around Shirley's age hoped their little girl could also board the band wagon to stardom. Besides trading, Cameron's other claim to fame was its excellent location for filming many of Hollywood's early productions. By the Christmas before I was three, my mother had taught me to recite Clement Moore's "The Night Before Christmas" in its entirety. Everyone thought that was quite marvelous and so it was suggested that I perform at the upcoming Christmas party.

The best part was that Samuel Goldman (or some other Hollywood big wig) would be in attendance and would probably beg my parents to sign a contract so he could use my phenomenal talents. The time came and Mother pushed me front and center and told me to say my poem. Instead of heeding her plea I stomped my feet and yelled. "The Night Before Christmas! I am tired of saying that dammed thing and I am not going to do it again--ever." Exit--stage right and the end of a movie career which never began. As I said before I don't recall any of this, but I do know that a few years ago it resurfaced in my brain when our great grandson Jayden was literally forced to learn the "damned thing" for a school assignment. I was able to sit in the back of the classroom and mouth the words to him every time he got a bit lost. We earned an A for his performance.

My husband and I have been competing to see who required the most medical attention lately. How blessed we are compared to all those years ago at the Trading Post. The nearest hospital for the Navajo was fifty miles away at Tuba City, but that wasn't much of a problem. They were not going to go there anyhow. As we have mentioned before, any structure in which a person expired was deemed a "ghost house" and never used again. The Bureau of Indian Affairs didn't quite go along with this belief--even the government is not so extravagant with our tax money that it is going to abandon a hospital each time it loses a patient.

The old generation of Navajo were not about to enter a building which was inhabited by the "chindi" of the departed. The local medicine man reigned supreme, and his curing ceremonies did seem to work quite well. There was also a public health nurse whose main occupation was frustration over how little cooperation she received for her suggestions on such things as personal hygiene, proper nutrition, and even birth control. It never entered her mind that a fifty-gallon barrel of water was a week's supply for most families. Her one big success was during a pandemic of sorts. An outbreak of typhoid or maybe it was diphtheria--one of those diseases we seldom think about today, took the life of several little ones and the good nurse was able to persuade the tribe that the white man had the answer to preventing more such tragedy. Old Hosteen Gishibetoh, who was considered the leading elder in our parts, allowed her to inoculate him and we soon had a line awaiting her ministrations. I was not pleased when my mother placed my pale face in that line and then returned to a very busy day at the store. There was no paperwork, no questions about allergies, just an agonizing jab in the upper arm. I spent the next two days wishing my left arm would fall off.

Three years ago today, God and our children provided this manufactured "hogan" we love so dearly. One hundred twenty years ago today my children's maternal grandmother made her debut in Petersburg, Pennsylvania. How she came from there to the trading post at Kaibeto some thirty-four years later will never be quite clear, but once there she never wanted to be anywhere else. The Navajo people of that era were gentle, generous, and trusting. Alas, as with any culture, there were a few rotten apples in the barrel. Because of intense clan and family pride, those sorts were referred to as someone who acts as if he has no relatives.

I was away at college when Mother, who was a rather shy lady, starred in an incident that was picked up by the "moccasin telegraph" and shared around every campfire from Tuba City to Navajo Mountain. One afternoon when the post was very busy, a young man who had obviously been sampling the local "firewater," (more about that in another story) began making a very unNavajo nuisance of himself. Daddy told him to take his obscenities and rough manner outside.

When the young man refused, Daddy took hold of his arm, intending to give the fellow a little help to finding some fresh air. The unthinkable happened and Daddy found himself on the floor, twisted in such a way that any self-defense was impossible. This altercation just happened to take place next to the counter under which axe handles were stored. It took Mother less than a second to grab one of those new axe handles and give the fellow such an embarrassing thrashing that he probably shopped at Shonto for the rest of his life. He didn't know how blessed he was that we always sold axe heads and axe handles separately. Seeing someone manhandle her man might have clouded Mother's judgment a bit when it came to choosing a proper weapon.

From that day forward, among other traders, Mother became known as "Axe Handle Julia." The Navajo, who always called her "Hosteen's Wife" or "Little Sister" gave her their silent approval and never changed her name at all. HAPPY HEAVENLY BIRTHDAY, MOTHER. You have been gone for a bit more than 38 years, but I still write this with tears running down my face.

Considered a sacred place by the Navajo, Navajo Mountain, north of Kaibeto was an always present reminder of the beauty of that area. There was a trading post there also, but Barry, the fellow who owned it, wasn't around all that much. His main residence was in Phoenix, but he did stop by to visit us occasionally. Barry's favorite activity was to join the yearly mule train which consisted of the mules used for the Grand Canyon tourist excursions. This long trek took several days, and the group always spent one night at Kaibeto where they enjoyed Mother's pinto beans, cornbread, and leg of lamb.

Barry and his pals were as Republican as Daddy was Democrat, and the political discussions went far into the night. They all bedded down in our living room to sleep beneath one of my parent's prize possessions which was a smiling portrait of Franklin D Roosevelt. Daddy enjoyed his repartee with Barry but once remarked to us that he hoped Barry never tried to run for public office because his ideas were pretty crazy, and he really should be paying more attention to his trading post.

I hadn't seen Barry in a long while when we ran into each under unusual circumstances. It was my senior year in high school, and the annual Freedom Foundation awards were televised in Phoenix. I had won a bobby pin sized trophy for an editorial I had written in the Winslow High Bulldog Barks. I have forgotten what Barry's award was, but it must have been pretty important for they saved him for last and gave him a long introduction. When he stepped in front of the camera, he didn't wait for the host to finish introducing us, but pronounced, "Oh, I already know this girl and I have spent many a night sleeping at her house--ER--on the floor-ah--I mean in the living room." The further it went the worse it got while seventeen-year-old me prayed the TV studio would collapse around us. My only consolation was that Winslow as yet did not have TV and my friends would not be witnessing this most embarrassing moment.

Revenge came quite a few years later when my first husband, our nine-month-old daughter, and I ran into Barry while shopping at a drugstore in Prescott. By this time Barry really was enjoying quite a political career and he seemed delighted to see us. Back then it was popular for politicians to kiss every baby they ran across, so of course our dear friend couldn't wait to get his hands on SueAnne. She was not inclined to go to strangers and pushed back toward me, pulling her plastic pants (anyone remember those?) askew which rendered them useless when Barry pulled her toward him. She left a lovely puddle down the front of him! By the way, Barry's last name was Goldwater.

Sometime during the thirties, the Bureau of Indian Affairs built a small two room school directly behind our trading post. It also housed whatever poor beleaguered teacher found herself in the position of school marm. None of these ladies were married and perhaps had shown some ineptitude in their employment and thus were sent to a place where they could cause no further problem. For certain, what they all had in common was total ignorance of the Navajo culture and language.

Back in those times it was thought that the sooner we made speaking English the only option available to Native Americans the better. No thought was given to some sort of methodology to accomplish this miracle. Teachers arrived with Dick and Jane and Puff and Spot and the expectation that every Navajo child would soon be saying, "Look, look. See Spot run," just like the Anglo children. The day school idea didn't work well anyhow for attendance was always sporadic. When your hogan is ten miles away and transportation consists of pony or wagon, tardiness was the order of the day. It was also thought that each child should be showered and then dressed in government provided clothing before proper lessons could begin. At least the BIA was wise enough to always hire a young Navajo couple to help with all this preparation. The poor teacher still struggled and, with a couple of exceptions, none lasted more than one year.

One of those exceptions was Mrs. Williams, a widow lady from Tucson. A spicy old gal, she didn't give a hoot about Dick and Jane and invented all sorts of ways to bridge the communications gap. She didn't care if she couldn't understand the kids or they her, she just loved them. She also loved the solitude of our location and our little family. She and mother had their own private book club and read everything from "Gone with the Wind" to "God's Little Acre." Of course you know how this tale is going to end. Much to her disgruntlement, disgust and horror, the BIA transferred Mrs. Williams. She was so angry that the day she left we were startled by a loud pounding on the back door. There she stood, gasping for breath from her effort to push a government issue bookcase, much admired by Mother, across our sandy yard. She told us the BIA would never miss it and she wanted Mother to have it. Stolen goods accepted, she and Mother exchanged a last hug. And that is why to this day the most well-built piece of furniture we "own" has PROPERTY OF US GOVT stamped on its back.

Not often, but every once in a while, my daddy could be downright ornery. One morning another one of the day school teachers desperately pounded on our back door tearfully asking for Mother's advice. One of her students had drawn a very detailed and a bit more anatomically correct than necessary picture of a nude male. Poor Miss Moore, who had no idea how to handle the situation, was wringing her hands and in a state of apoplexy. The Navajo were and still are an extremely modest people. But when a dozen family members live together in an area the size of most Anglo kitchens, children are bound to see a few things we whites would think unseemly. Mother tried to explain to Miss Moore that the child had probably drawn the picture in all innocence, never dreaming she would think he had done something bad.

Before Mother could finish calming the poor distraught maiden lady, my dad, who had just taken a bathroom break, appeared at the sink to wash his hands. That may sound odd, but our bathroom sink was actually in what passed for our dining room. (Another story for sure.) Curious about what was causing all the commotion, Daddy took the liberty of picking up the picture, causing Miss Moore even more distress. After studying it for a second, he said, "Miss Moore, you being an unmarried lady and all, I don't understand how you even know what this is or why it upsets you." Grabbing the offending work of art out of Daddy's hand, face and neck glowing red, poor Miss Moore literally ran back to the schoolhouse. I don't think Mother spoke to Daddy for the rest of that day. I am not sure Miss Moore ever spoke to him again.

The Navajo had one belief that I always thought was unfortunate. It was considered extremely bad luck to be in the same area with a son-in-law. That meant there was no relationship at all between the two except fear of seeing each other. So, if Mrs. Manygoats was in the midst of trying to decide between a can of Carnation milk or a can of Pet Milk, but suddenly threw her Pendleton blanket/shawl over her head and made a run for the door, you knew without looking that her son-in-law had also arrived to do some shopping. All we could do was push her grocery choices to one side to await her return. That would not happen until he had his fill of "total chosie", treated his horse to a bag of oats, decided whether to purchase one or two plugs of tobacco and maybe even bought a new pair of Levi's.

Since Navajo sheep camps were often located in the same proximity with other family members, I often wondered how that worked out. There was no such taboo between mother-in-law and daughter-in-law. This son-in-law belief must have challenged the Navajo custom of always sharing whatever one had.

One of my sons-in-law drove all the way across the Valley this morning so he and my "baby" could spend a couple of social distance hours with us. The other son-in-law brought flowers on Friday (along with his wife, of course). These two men have enriched my life for many years, and I can't imagine not being able to communicate with them. My husband has a nearly hundred-year-old mother-in-law left over from his first marriage. This week we had a letter from Marge telling us how much she still thought about us and cared for us. Sometimes we white folk do get our priorities in the proper order! Happy Mother's Day to all and may we moms never forget to honor those good sons-in-law.

My mother swore me to secrecy on this tale, but enough time has passed, and circumstances have changed so drastically, that I can see no harm in "letting the cat (in this case, the body) out of the bag." I also found mention of the incident in a book written by one of the Richardson brothers.

During the pandemic of the Spanish flu, the trader who was then at Kaibeto unfortunately passed away in the living quarters. His wife, knowing that if the Navajo found out that someone had died in the building, would never enter it again, locked up everything until she could send a rider bearing the sad news to some relatives in Tuba City. When this message reached the dead trader's younger brother, he hurriedly procured a "touring car" and by three o'clock the next morning had smuggled his brother's body away.

This all happened in 1919, some fifteen years before my parents appeared on the Kaibeto scene. Even so, I feel it is worth mentioning for a couple of reasons. I was married before Mother ever told me this story, along with the aforementioned secrecy clause, because she said that even then, if word got out, it could ruin our livelihood. This shows how deeply ingrained the belief about the "chindi" of the dead was planted in the Navajo culture. It is also a tale of our own times and what we are experiencing now. It is very unlikely that poor trader ever had a proper burial service and even more likely that the courageous wife had to carry on alone to keep the post running until new management could be found. Tomorrow I will talk about how my parents came to be in charge of Kaibeto and I assure you that is a much happier tale.

My parents met and fell in love at the wonderful little "off reservation" spot on Highway 89A North called Cameron. My dad's mother worked there as the hotel hostess and my mother was one of her associates. The proper terms would probably be head hotel maid and plain hotel maid. This is my parents love story, so forgive me for glamorizing a bit.

My father came west to visit his mom and the way the story was always told to me was that he took one look at the lovely dark eyed, brunette part Iroquois assistant and declared "That is the woman I am going to marry." There may have been a little more to it than that. My grandmother had managed to marry off five of her six surviving children and was probably wondering why this eldest son, now in his early forties, was not settling down and providing grandchildren. Since he had shown absolutely no inclination toward matrimony up to this point, it makes sense that there was some sort of encouraging influence.

This was still the time of the Great Depression, so "happily ever after" usually came with a catch or two. I am sure that Daddy was in dire need of a job, and it appears Mr. Richardson, who owned Kaibeto at the time, was weary of running out of family and friends to staff one of his most desolate posts, and Daddy was willing and able. No festive ceremony marked the occasion and with only a marriage license from the courthouse in Phoenix, it appears the newlyweds may have spent their honeymoon in a tent pitched between a very run down Kaibeto Trading Post and the mesa it depended on to keep it stable.

Julia Jones, as a young married in 1934, waiting as the trading post is remodeled.

It was decided that the bride should be kept in the manner in which she was accustomed, and this included indoor plumbing and a kitchen with running water. There are quite a few pictures of the resulting renovations with the bride looking reasonably happy. It is what these pictures don't show that is amazing. A great deal of excavation would have been needed to add on the required amenities, but nothing like a backhoe is ever present. I don't know for sure, but I am almost certain that a great many Navajo men and a great many shovels were involved.

The things that keep me awake at night! Last night as I was mentally reviewing the layout of our trading post living quarters, it occurred to me that our kitchen should have been filled with water each time we had a decent rain. As noted yesterday, once it was decided to add on to the original building, a lot of digging had to be done. At some point someone decided enough sand had been removed to make space for a bathroom and kitchen. Walls were cemented almost to the top except where a row of windows were installed. When all was said and done the bottom of the windows ended up being level with the ground. This resulted in a huge slope of a yard with the lowest point ending by the kitchen door.

My memory fails me here. Perhaps we just knew better than to open the kitchen door when it rained. One had to step down to enter the kitchen from outside and then step up again to enter where the old structure connected with new. Same with the bathroom which really wasn't a bathroom at all for it never contained a bathtub. Aside from the obvious piece of equipment, the room was outfitted only with a pipe which dispensed cold water. Maybe someone intended to install a sink there one day, but the sink ended up in a quaint little room that was part of the original building.

This room was little more than a hallway between the old living room and the new kitchen. The enormous sink fit okay but was visible from any part of the living room. Once you used the bathroom, in order to wash your hands or anything else, it was necessary to step out of the bathroom, step down into the kitchen, navigate that space, then step up into the funny little room and perform your ablutions in full view of anyone who happened to be in the living room. Or you could go the opposite direction which meant you stepped up into the only bedroom and wended your way around the furniture in the living room before entering the sink room. Of course the sink was cold water only, but it did have a nice little ledge to hold the bowl where Daddy's dentures spent each night.

The door to the trading post was at the far end of the living room and one had to make three big steps down in order to enter there. Between trading post and warehouse there was another foot and half drop. Round and round we went, day after day, never missing a step and not giving a thought to our quadruple level existence. The only casualty we ever had was when our two-year-old fell down the steps from the living room and opened up quite a cut by his eye. He still guilt-trips me because I allowed the local Mormon Missionary, who had once been in training to be a doctor, tend to his wound. I keep telling him that the scar only adds to his rugged, manly charm.

Each Navajo family had at least three dogs, all of questionable breed, and every one of them earned their keep by being expert sheep herders. We didn't sell dog food. I doubt that it had been invented yet. So most of those dogs probably had a pretty good hunting instinct to supplement their diet.

I doubt the Navajos understood our relationship with our dogs who shared our lives and ate our vittles. One of them was Lollypop, a chubby little chihuahua given to me by Glenn, the son of the trader at Tonalea. Glenn never made it back from WWII and that is probably one of the reasons my parents tolerated Lollypop. From the time I received her, she became my baby. I constantly dressed her in doll clothing, wheeled her around in my doll carriage and put her to sleep at night in my doll bed. She put up with all this without a whimper or a growl. She adored me and mourned for days every fall when I became old enough to leave for school. She tolerated my mother and that was probably because she was smart enough not to bite the hand which fed her most of the time. Other than that, Lolly hated anything that breathed and moved, especially if it had two legs. Just entering the same room with her earned a person a snarling growl and a view of a mouthful of gleaming needle teeth.

Every once in a while, someone would forget to close the gate to our big yard and Lolly would go exploring. My discovery of her absence would be announced with screams and hysteria that disturbed the peace and tranquility for miles around. Daddy would call on Jack Hudson, who was not only our handyman, but also had the ability to track an animal or person many days after they had been in the area. In due time, here would come Jack, holding Lolly straight out as far as his arms could reach, while she hacked away at his shirt cuffs and glove tops. He would gently deposit Lolly behind the gate, double checking to make sure it was locked and report "mission accomplished" to Daddy. I suppose Daddy paid Jack a whole dollar for each day he worked--not bad wages for the time. I suspect that on "dog days" Jack may have gone back to his hogan with several silver dollars in each pocket.

Wool season usually started about the time I got home from school in the spring. I never got to see much of the shearing, but my impression was that it only took a few minutes for the fellow wielding the shears to finish the job and then reach for another disgruntled sheep. All this wool was then stuffed into a gigantic gunny sack provided by the trader and then transported by pickup or wagon to the nearest trading post. Each of these sacks could hold between 250 to 300 pounds of wool that were weighed outside on an enormous scale. There was always quite an audience for this event and every trader was center stage.

Not often, but once in a while, one of the sacks would weigh in quite a bit over 300 pounds and then the drama would begin. Out would come

Sacks of wool stacked 4+ high—each weighing 200 pounds—from sheep at shearing season of spring 1953, awaiting transport from Kaibeto. Julia Jones stands atop.

Daddy's pocketknife and a huge surgery would immediately be performed. The "patient" usually had one of three conditions. The wool would be soggy and wet. The wool would be liberally laced with sand. Or the most terminal and hardest to deal with, the wool would be interspersed with a great many small stones and pebbles. There were never any hard feelings, and audience and trader alike would have a good laugh. Daddy would state how much weight he was going to deduct, plus a small amount for our faithful Jack Hudson to "cure" the condition by removing the foreign bodies and resacking the wool.

Back inside the store, Daddy would bring out the account of how much the seller owed from his winter of trading and deduct the wool price. There was seldom anything left over and if there was, it was usually traded on the spot for flour, coffee, and other staples. The Navajo had to have absolute trust in the honesty of the trader, and I am proud to say my daddy had one of the best reputations on the Rez. He didn't mind playing the game, but he never played to win. Tomorrow we will find out about what happened to all that wool.

The wool sack population grew quickly and soon there were as many as fifty piled by the trading post front door. Each one bore a large KTP (for Kaibeto Trading Post) along with its weight in giant black letters. That stack of sacks was a wonderful lounging place for all the husbands who waited for wives to complete their shopping. What better vantage place to catch sight of your mother-in-law in plenty of time to slip away before she spotted you? At night it was a star gazer's dream for me as I reclined on the topmost bag and watched the heavens ever revolving majesty. All very romantic, but those sacks also represented the survival of our enterprise and had to be sold for a profit.

Daddy then had one of his biggest challenges before him. In order to contact a buyer and secure the best price possible, he had to use the telephone. Trading posts were the only places having phones. I am not sure how many posts shared our line, but at least a dozen. Each post had its own "ring" (ours was a long-short-long) and of course your ring sounded at the same time in every other post along the way. Those of you who ever had a party line might have some idea of this if you quadruple the possible complications.

The phone looked like a wooden box with a mouthpiece sticking out in front and a receiver attached to the side. There was also a little handle on the side for cranking out whatever ring you wanted. One very long crank was supposed to alert the operator from Flagstaff. Daddy would start there, hoping to reach his buyer. This worked about five percent of the time. Once this minor miracle was achieved, he had to make himself understood. This was achieved by inhaling until his face was purple and then shouting until both eyes were dangerously protruding. Once the price he was going to be paid was settled, that was it. There was no contract to be signed or other legal considerations. A simple gentleman's agreement sufficed to guarantee our business would survive another year.

Jean DeJolie is on my mind today. I didn't know Jean, but as one of five elderly Navajo ladies pictured on Facebook yesterday that DeJolie name means that I knew a great many of her family. Perhaps the Bob DeJolie I knew was her grandfather. Or there is a slight possibility she was one of the only two girls born into the DeJolie family after twelve boys.

The DeJolies were one of those families with a surname that obviously had been handed out to them somewhere along the way as they struggled with the white man's idea of civilizing and controlling Native Americans. DeJolie was definitely a unique name for a Navajo. Their eldest son, born about 1934 was Charley and ended up graduating from the University of New Mexico. This was after he had graduated from Exeter Academy in New Hampshire with full scholarship. I think the next son was Harry and he is the father of award-winning photographer LeRoy DeJolie. Almost every year when I returned home from school, I would be greeted by a new DeJolie--always male. My mother and Mrs. DeJolie always seemed to think this was hilarious. I do know there were a full dozen boys before one of Daddy's letters mentioned that Mrs. DeJolie had given birth to a girl, and he figured that production would now cease. If I remember correctly there was yet another girl after that and then one more boy.

Sadly, the point of all this is that I can only speculate on where Jean DeJolie fits into the DeJolie family tree. Her picture was there yesterday because she is one of those who succumbed to the virus. So I memorialize her and honor her as representative of all the grandchildren and great grandchildren of those I have been writing about. May God keep them safe, along with those few elders who were there when I was.

Names--we all have trouble remembering them, putting the right face to the correct name, etc. The old time Navajo got around all that by believing that it was bad luck to call each other by name. If I were conversing with a Navajo friend and wanted to mention my father, I would not say "Hosteen Jones went to buy sheep today." Even though Hosteen was a term of respect, it would have been more respectful and better manners to say, "That man, who is my father, went to buy sheep today".

This bit of Navajo etiquette caused something of a problem when it came to keeping accounts at the trading post. We really needed to keep accurate track of who was charging all that hay and canned tomatoes and yards of velvet. By the time my parents took over Kaibeto, most accounts did have names attached, but there were a few among the very elderly who still refused to tell us their names. Out of respect for their advanced ages, none of their relatives would divulge them either.

Daddy solved the problem by tagging them with one of their physical characteristics or something from their lifestyle. Thus, we had "Lady Big Nose" who although bent with age and tiny in stature had inherited a stately nose befitting a high-ranking chief. We also had "Old Joe on Top", a sweet natured and very elderly man who chose to live alone in his hogan which was situated on top of our very near mesa. Obviously, "Hosteen Smallpox" had the scars from a childhood bout with that insidious disease and "Missing Fingers" had once upon a time been careless while chopping wood. These names were given thoughtfully and respectfully with no intention of teasing or ridicule. I doubt the recipients ever figured out how we kept them all straight.

One other part of the Navajo culture which would have stood them in good stead today was that hand shaking or embracing when meeting was not considered good manners. Out of respect for the white man's culture a, Navajo would softly clasp your hand when you offered it. Eye contact was also considered bad manners. Emily Post would have left in a hurry had she ever visited us. Thank God we have figured out that a lot of Emily's rules were nonsense, and we are realizing the Navajo culture was far more considerate of our human state.

I am looking at them now--a bit lumpy, definitely crooked with uneven edges, tightly woven in some places and too loose in others. They have been with me since childhood and one of them was just the perfect size to cover my "Monkey Ward's" doll bed. This trio is one of many "starter rugs" Daddy bought from beginning weavers. All traders bought rugs from Navajo weavers, and some were magnificent in design, perfectly symmetrical and feasts for the soul. Many others were saddle blankets which were nicely woven, colorfully striped but with no particular design.

Navajo rugs from the Kaibeto Trading Post, given to Suzanne Purdy (Langford) by her uncle Ralph Jones in the early 1950s. From the collection of Peter Langford.

If I remember correctly, saddle blankets had to be exactly 36 inches by 32 inches. I do remember that the big yard stick was always involved when we bought one. They accumulated quickly and Mr. Richardson at Cameron was always glad to get them as the tourists who stopped there snapped them up almost as soon as they arrived. A tightly woven saddle blanket with correct dimensions brought the weaver $3.00. One not quite so pristine might only bring $2.00. The beauties could take more than a half day of dickering, but I don't remember any of them ever earning the weaver more than $20.00.

Those great weavers had to start somewhere, so I am almost sure that every trader did as my parents did and encouraged little girls by purchasing their sometimes downright ugly first attempts at the loom. The quarter they received would buy a nice box of Crackerjack and several days' supply of penny candy. Mother could never bear to throw one of these creations away. She used them everywhere like the crocheted doilies popular in Anglo homes during those days. We gave them to visiting relatives who seemed to view them as the treasures they were.

Of my three surviving rugs, two are gracing my houseplant collection and one (the doll bed one) covers a foot stool. They defy their almost eighty years of existence by looking exactly as they always have. After the husband and the dog, they just might be the things I would grab if this place ever caught on fire!

Every trading post was also a pawn shop. At Kaibeto, squash blossom necklaces, concho belts, and strands of coral beads all nested with each other in a big white cupboard located next to the penny candy and Baby Ruth bars. For some pieces that cupboard was almost a permanent home, for as soon as Mrs. Nez or Hosteen Manygoats had sold their wool or lambs and paid to redeem their pawn, they had to again begin the process of feeding their family.

Those were the days when there was no worry about fake turquoise, and every necklace or belt was always worth far more than the dollar amount held against them. There was a rule, or perhaps it was a real legislated law, that the trader could not sell any pawned item until it had been housed for a full year. Daddy paid not the slightest attention to this and as long as the jewelry owner was alive he or she had no fear of his precious heirloom being sold. Some of the pieces were in there so long, it would have taken a week of polishing to remove the tarnish.

When someone died without redeeming their jewelry, Daddy always made sure there was no family member who wanted to redeem it. Due to the "chindi" belief, it was very rare to have someone want a dead relative's necklace, no matter how little owed. Then and only then, would he offer it to one of our visiting relatives or friends and never for more than the amount owed. Pawning was definitely not one of our more profitable efforts. An interesting sideline is mainly what it was.

When Jim and I retired we moved to a location only a few miles from the Rez. One day a Kaibeto lady came by our place and wanted to pawn her squash blossom necklace for two hundred dollars. Even though I wasn't sure of the authenticity of the piece, the trader in me just couldn't turn her down. Weeks turned into years, and Jim kept telling me to see if I could sell the necklace. One day as I returned from a visit with our Phoenix family, my husband sheepishly handed me $200.00. It seemed Mrs. Sly had come by for her necklace with no apologies, taking it for granted it would still be there. Guess she figured "daughter like father." It gave me a good feeling and I didn't even say "I told you so." (At least not very loud.)

Senator Goldwater was not the only celebrity to visit our trading post. Several years after WWII a Navajo fellow named Carl Gorman was a frequent visitor. Over grazing was always a problem in our area and Carl had some sort of job with the BIA which required him to visit around the Rez and make sure no Navajo was in possession of more than the approved number of livestock. Carl had a son named Rudy who was a couple years older than I and sometimes Carl would drop him off to spend the day with us while he worked. Rudy and I were not that compatible as all he wanted to do was draw pictures on the cardboard sections out of candy bar boxes which Daddy saved for him. He could not understand why I couldn't just pick up a pencil, as he did, and make magical designs and life-like drawings of people and animals. If we played in the plentiful sand in the yard, I was content to make hills and valleys and roads for my toy cars. Rudy made Taj Mahals and castles complete with moats.

Losing patience with me one day, Rudy started giving me lessons on how to whistle. From the beginning I was a pretty apt student, and Rudy had a whole afternoon for pursuing his artistic endeavors. That was before I figured out that one could whistle and be a pest at the same time.

Rudy often left me a drawing or two, and I filed them away with my paper dolls and other important possessions. After a while, his father Carl was transferred, so Rudy didn't come any more. Next time I saw him we were in the same writing class at NAU (Arizona State Teacher's College back then). He was active in the Drama Club, and I was busy playing the flute, so our paths didn't cross often. By now you have probably guessed this one. Rudy was none other than RC Gorman who has paintings in high places in Washington D. C. and all over the world. What happened to those cardboard drawings he gave me? I tossed them along with other childish things when I went away to college.

Having known Rudy makes me wonder a couple of things. If he hadn't taught me the joy of making pretty music with my lips, would I have ever fallen in love with the flute? More important, if I had kept those drawings, would my children have had a much easier time paying for their educations? Rudy died maybe as much as ten years ago in Taos, New Mexico, where he had lived for many years.

One of you did a bit of research yesterday and found out that the Carl Gorman I mentioned had been one of the original Code Talkers who used the Navajo language to communicate our military's secret messages. The enemy never broke the code. I am not sure how, but we always knew that Mr. Gorman was a Code Talker. We knew of no others.

When WWII became a horrible reality, many young Navajo men volunteered. I say volunteered because if memory serves correctly, there were very few ways back then for the "Your Uncle Sam Wants You" greeting to reach native Americans. Not all of them returned. Sadly, because they had married in traditional Navajo ceremonies, their widows could not collect benefits.

When the war was finally over many who returned carried souvenirs which ended up in our trading post. It seems that while they were among their Anglo comrades those Navajo fellows forgot their heritage for a bit and wanted to bring home the same stuff everyone else carted off the battle fields. A few days of the tranquility and tradition of the Navajo culture soon cured the urge, and we had a huge box of everything from helmets to bayonets hidden in the dark corner behind the horse bridles and leather goods. Daddy, a WWI vet who really didn't like any of that stuff, freely handed them out to any visiting relative or friend who had a hankering after such things.

Of the many Navajos who left for the war, only one named Dale signed up for another tour of duty. He always paid us a visit during his furloughs. A few others, John comes to mind and another named Scott, never seemed properly settled back in their native environment.

Now skip ahead many years to a small group of slightly elderly former classmates from Winslow who decided a guided tour of Navajo land might be fun. There certainly wasn't much on that tour I hadn't experienced but the company was excellent, and I did want to see the new Navajo museum at Tuba City. That museum has an entire room dedicated to Code Talkers, including pictures of every one of them. And there they were--Dale, John, and Scott. All three had kept their secret for a lifetime simply because they had been told they must never tell anyone what they had done during the war. Thus today, I am not including last names because even though they are no longer here, they do have descendants in that area, and it seems right to preserve the illusion they lived with all their hearts. I wish they had lived long

You'll Like Arizona

THIS little committee-of-one will welcome you to Kaibito trading post, on the Navajo Indian Reservation near Tonalea, Arizona. She is our first reason for congratulating the manager of the post, who is her father. The second reason is the exclusive use of Standard Gasoline there.

MCCANN-ERICKSON. INC., SAN FRANCISCO

Printed in U. S. A.

Elizabeth Anne in her Navajo dress, belt, and necklace posing at the Kaibeto gas pump for a 1939 Standard Oil Company ad, the gasoline available at the trading post. *Used with permission* enough to witness this time when the few remaining Code Talkers are given the honor and respect they so deserve. We very well may owe them our lives.

I mentioned yesterday that Navajo WWII widows could not collect benefits because they were married in a traditional Navajo ceremony and could not produce a certificate of marriage that would be honored by the state. There was one exception, a couple named Silas. Fern did make the journey to Flagstaff and before Silas shipped out, they were legally Mr. and Mrs. Lefthand. Silas gave his life for his country, and his relatives benefited every month thereafter. Like all traditional Navajo people, Fern shared whatever she possessed. She never risked losing her benefits by marrying again. She probably could have rewed in the Navajo way as our government could not possibly have considered her married, could it?

A gentle lady with a sweet smile, Fern endeared herself to us through our many years in the trading business. The day after my daddy died, although he had been retired for some years, I wrote a quick note to the current Kaibeto trader, asking him to spread the word. At the end of Daddy's funeral service, there was Fern and a substantial number of her family, all dressed in their traditional best, as they filed by Daddy's casket. My mother and I had managed to hold back our tears, but not after that moment. To show their respect for my father, that family had left Kaibeto long before dawn to reach Cottonwood and then put aside their ingrained reluctance to be under the same roof with a dead person. No memorial could have been more meaningful, no eulogy more plainly stated. I pray you all have such a moment to treasure this Memorial Day weekend as we go about the business of remembering and honoring our departed loved ones.

The fall I was supposed to enter third grade, my Aunt Zada needed a serious surgery and was not able to care for me. Thus, one of the first experiments in home schooling was born. Winslow provided all the appropriate textbooks, Mother purchased a couple of those big red Indian Chief note pads, and the trading post donated some of its many number two lead pencils. A small table and a chair were placed by the door between our living quarters and the store so mother could easily reach me for tutoring purposes. She seldom made it up those three steps to our living room, but I sneaked down them at every opportunity.

Feeling only slightly guilty, I learned how to saw off a one eighth part of a bale of hay and how to measure the right amount of oats to put in a feed bag. I finally figured out how to make change for a dollar without using the coin depressions in the cash drawer for "cheat sheets". On our old-fashioned balance scales, I learned how to weigh everything from penny candy to potatoes. I was instructed on how to put cans on shelves facing outward so they looked nice and how to measure fabric by the yard or half yard. I could draw a pint of kerosene or white gas from the proper barrel. Although Mother frowned on it, if we were busy, I would sneak outside with the big steel handle which attached to our lone gas pump and pump up the number of gallons requested. I made good use of the "church key" opener to punch open the many cans of motor oil we sold. Cutting a plug of tobacco into halves or fourths was also mastered, along with learning the difference between bias tape and rick rack. I either had to make change for all these transactions or enter them in the charge ledger.

Finally, and most important, I learned for sure where babies came from. One afternoon I heard cries of anguish and moaning coming from behind the big woodpile just south of the gas pump. When I started out the door to see what sort of trouble this meant, Mother yanked me back inside so hard and fast I feared my arm would come off. Two hours later young Mrs. Tsosie appeared in the "bull pen" with a brand-new baby for all of us of to admire.

Mother had told me that babies came from under the rocks up on the mesa. Now that I knew they came from behind the woodpile, I decided if Mother didn't even know for sure where babies came from, she probably didn't know very much about that stuff I was supposed to be learning from all those books. I stopped feeling that tiny bit of guilt over not studying and enjoyed the rest of Indian Trading 101 which lasted for an entire happy semester.

I suppose I am one of the few people living today who actually remembers Pearl Harbor. It was a beautiful Sunday. The trading post was closed, and we drove to Grey Mountain Trading Post to visit friends. When we arrived, all the ladies were crying, the men were looking angry, and no one paid a lick of attention to me. Soon Mother started to cry too. I had never seen adult women cry before, nor was I used to being placed on the back burner. Mrs. Reed, the trader's wife, had always treated me as if she had birthed me herself, but not on that day. It was one of the most frightening moments of my life. I wish I could recall how it came to be, but I do know that by the time we climbed back in our faithful little red Buick I again felt secure and safe.

I have almost no memory of the war itself. Children my age were insulated from such things, and the only way the war touched us was the "fun" stuff like peeling the foil off gum wrappers and taking it to toss in a box at the drugstore. We received great praise when we saved a quarter to buy a stamp toward purchasing a war bond to help the war effort, but we had no idea what the term "war effort" meant.

Meanwhile, back at the trading post, Daddy began flying the US flag. There was a little nub of a hill not far from the woodpile and that was where he chose to display Old Glory. It was a real hefty, full-size flagpole and its installation must have required the help of several other men. (I missed out on a lot of important stuff by having to go off to school in Winslow.) For many years, one of his first chores in the morning was to run the flag up the pole and he never failed to take it down before dark. When I was home, I always enjoyed running alongside him as he went to perform this important rite.

I never saw him salute the flag nor was he picky about how it was folded. His thing was to never, ever, ever let it touch the ground. He was so serious about this infraction that I never got up the nerve to ask him what would happen if the flag should so much as brush the dusty earth. My son now has the flag which draped Daddy's coffin, and his good wife has seen to it that it is still folded and displayed properly. For however many generations that flag graces us children should be told that it must never, never come in contact with the ground!

Most everything was rationed during WWII, and that included many of the staples on trading post shelves. You would have to be a bit older than I (and who will admit to that?) to recall how it all worked. I will take a guess and say that merchants were allowed goods according to the amount of ration stamps they sent to suppliers. My parents received ration books of course, and even a few of our Navajo customers found themselves possessing the little volume containing several different categories of stamps. Mostly the government sat and scratched its head over how to distribute the cute little books. Knowing that the Tallsalt's hogan was located right before the turnoff to Navajo Mountain and that the Bigman's sheep camp was over the hill next to the windmill was what constituted an address in our part of the world.

Perhaps the census of 1940 was consulted because any Navajo who allowed himself to be found would have used the trading post for an address. The result was a huge gap in what was needed and what my folks received. I have no idea how other trading posts survived, but Mother's retelling of those times makes sense. Sugar and meat were two of the scarcest items, but somehow syrup and jelly kept coming and became acceptable substitutes for the Navajo sweet tooth.

The meat problem was the most easily solved. It didn't take long for everyone to figure out that Uncle Sam had no way of knowing how much meat was being butchered on the Rez. When brought to the trading post to be sold (a perfectly normal part of trading) the meat was also traded for stamps for much needed items like shoes, or sugar and maybe even a tire or two. I won't mention who the brokers for these transactions might have been, but I do remember that friends and relatives in Winslow had a higher protein diet during those years than most of the rest of the country.

When I was eleven my Grandma Houck (Mother's mother) accompanied by my twelve-year-old cousin Fay came from Pennsylvania for the summer. I didn't know either one of them well, but Fay and I took one look at each other and decided we were twins. Perhaps because we looked a bit alike or smelled somewhat the same, even "scissors jaw" Lollypop liked Fay and never once bared her teeth in Fay's direction. Grandma was not so lucky and spent a great deal of her time anxiously guarding her cotton stockinged ankles and even her feet which were encased in black grannie shoes favored by elderly ladies of that day.

In no time at all I had given Fay the tour of all my favorite hideouts and mysterious little paths which went here and there and nowhere. One afternoon, heading back from one of those excursions we discovered a slight bend in the "big wash" where we could see nearly all the way back to the trading post, but no one could see us. After a little poking around we also realized that the sandstone shoring up this location was extremely soft and would be easy to dig. Since privacy was nonexistent at the trading post, we decided to excavate our own little private cave. We "borrowed" a couple of Mother's gardening implements and in less than two days our little home away from adults was ready.

It was large enough for us to be seated comfortably and went at least five feet straight back. We carefully carved out shelves where we installed a few items we borrowed (stole) from home and store. Candles and candy bars and animal crackers were definitely necessary amenities. Our lovely little den was so close to the road we could feel the vibrations from the horses and wagons and pickup trucks when they drove down the road before crossing the wash. We thought this was deliciously fun. (Would you believe that we were both excellent students?)

One late afternoon when we had both been a bit too engrossed in Carolyn Keene's latest Nancy Drew Mystery, we looked up and there stood

Grandma Houck. I didn't think anyone could possibly navigate past the front gate wearing those grandma shoes, but she had obviously tracked us right up that sand strewn wash to the door of our lair. Fay and I both waited for a tongue lashing about the evils of stealing and hiding our ill-gotten gain. Instead, she looked at our establishment for a few moments, shook her head slightly and reminded us it was close to supper time and we had better get along home right then as she was almost certain the store was already closed. The trading post was not closed when we returned but I gave it no thought.

The next morning we found our den had caved in on itself, leaving scarcely any evidence of its existence. What has always puzzled me is how the Nancy Drew books, brass candle holder and garden trowels we left behind when Grandma came to get us turned up at the trading post a couple of days later.

The case of the quivering wool pile! When Joe Many Mules could not cram another ounce of wool into the big burlap sacks Daddy provided, he placed the leftovers in an old flour sack or just pitched them into the back of his wagon. On reaching the trading post he was escorted into the warehouse where his burden was weighed and then tossed unto a huge pile of similar offerings. Getting that wool sacked was a year-round low priority task, and sometimes the fuzzy mountain grew nearly as high as my head. It also was an apt weather predictor. When the wool pile began to vibrate, we knew that before the afternoon ended we would be having a thunderstorm. If the quivering was accompanied by strange clicking noises, the storm was going to be a real gully washer. Even Nancy Drew might have been stymied by this phenomenon.

Before I was born, my parents purchased a six-week-old Pit Bull from the trader at Inscription House. "Eddie Girl" was meant to be a guard dog and was trained solely for that purpose. She did not like to be inside and spent most of her time keeping a sharp eye on our big yard. She never did turn into a Pit Bull, but instead looked exactly like "His Master's Voice", the RCA Victor dog which appeared on all their products. Unlike Lollypop who hated everyone, Eddie developed the ability to tell the difference between friend or foe. Her best and most valuable attribute was being able to tell the difference between a bull snake and a rattlesnake. She was absolutely fearless about cornering the latter until her unique "snake bark" alerted one of my parents. There were few worries about letting me play outside for as soon as I opened the door Eddie stayed by my side.

There was one exception to these heroics. As soon as Eddie felt the change in atmospheric pressure heralding a storm, she turned into a quaking, shaking, tooth rattling mass of canine anxiety. Bounding over a low section of fence, she would present herself in the bull pen until her frantic scratching persuaded someone to open the gate. From there she howled her way into the warehouse, not slowing a mite until she dove headfirst into the big pile of wool. All hints of storm passed for several hours before she took up her post again.

Many of you, including myself, have been wondering how all these old trading post stories have come into existence. They just seem to pop into my mind and I write them. Yesterday I found somewhat of an answer. I was looking for something else when I came across a large composition notebook filled with these tales and adventures. Every page is handwritten in my stellar Winslow grammar school penmanship, a project which would have required many hours to complete. I have absolutely no memory of creating this "almost book". It wasn't until the next to last page I spotted a clue to what might be the reason for this forgetfulness.

About a dozen years ago when Jim and I were living down the road from Navajo Trails Mission, I had the delightful experience of tutoring a young Navajo boy named Avery. Even though Avery was (and still is) a modern example of the Navajo tribe, I was so taken by him that I couldn't resist incorporating him into my writing. Recalling when I worked with Avery led me to realize that I had done all that writing shortly before our granddaughter Melissa suddenly died of heart failure. The shock of that event must have unwired my brain for all these years. Before finding that notebook, I was sure I was going to run out of stories before we ran out of pandemic That is doubtful now. So ahxe'e eh (close as I can come to spelling "thank you" in Navajo) to Avery for being such a great inspiration all those years ago. My sources tell me you have grown into a fine young man. As to Melissa, is it my imagination, or have you been peering over my shoulder lately? Whatever, tomorrow we will learn about fishing on the Rez.

I don't know if this memory should be called "Going Fishing" or "Sheep Watering," but first we have to get there and today that will take some serious effort. The unpaved road between Tonalea and Kaibeto was a perilous undertaking and your chances of reaching whichever of those two destinations you planned without mishap was about fifty-fifty. Even so, that Kaibeto Road, compared to the one to Frenchman's Lake (today's destination) was a modern freeway. Daddy's loyalty to the Buick family meant that our several mile journey from the "main road" to the lake was always horrific. The first mile consisted of three or four sand dunes. The poor Buick would shake and shudder and sometimes clear all of them as we held our respective breaths. Most often we had to dig the poor machine out at least once. With the dunes behind us, the trail turned into sheer rock navigated to the accompaniment of my mother screaming, "Ralph, we're going to break a spring--Ralph, slow down."

Mother Julia has caught a fish at a rare desert lake on Kaibito Creek at some distance from Kaibeto Trading Post, but worth the drive through desert and sand for some recreation and time away from a post that was, as Elizabeth Anne has noted, "a sunrise-to-sunset, all-week long venture". Not to mention a chance for some fresh food from a diet largely of canned products from the post's supply. – *circa 1952*

After such a tortuous ordeal by auto, one would think that arriving at Frenchman's Lake would be a joyous event. But no, the real effort had only begun. Carrying all our fishing gear and food supplies for the day, we had a half mile walk in deep sand until we reached a steep sandy incline which brought us within sight of the lake. This soupy little body of water was about the length of three football fields and perhaps a bit wider. We never knew its origins, but since its existence was dependent on an earthen dam at one end, we rather thought it was the result of one of the CCC (Civilian Conservation Corps) projects sponsored by the government shortly before WWII. The aroma close to the water left no doubt about its popularity with the local sheep.

We also had no information about the origin of the name, but we had been told by the trader at Tonalea that his predecessor was the one who had stocked it with bass and blue gill. The bass were a rare catch, but the blue gill had multiplied to the point that no offering was ever refused. In a very short time I would be bored by this repetitive sport and Nancy, George, Bess and I would seek a comfortable spot to spend the rest of the morning. It never failed that as soon as I had relocated, here came the sheep. When they crested the hill, they broke into a frantic run which culminated a foot or so onto the water's edge where they drank thirstily, happily pooping and peeing as they imbibed. Sometimes several bands arrived at the same time. While I renewed my resolve to never eat any of our catch, I was always fascinated when each herder gave his particular call and only his sheep separated from the grand mass and followed him or her. As Jesus liked to say, "My sheep know my voice".

Tomorrow we will find our way back to Kaibeto and you will learn of a bit of Arizona known by very few.

Yesterday we talked about how each of the sheep arriving at French-man's Lake, like the disciples of Christ, knew his own master's voice. This "sheep" also figured out the signs of preparation heralding our departure. I always tried to get a head start on my parents so as not to be laden with any of the paraphernalia we had carried in, and which now was enlarged by a wet gunny sack of fish. (I really was not a very nice kid which is why a couple of my cousins called me "Brat.")

The climb to the car was a grueling two step forward and one step back ordeal through the sand which proved that none of us had any sort of heart problem. The way back to the Kaibeto Road was an easier downhill stretch but did make it evident that General Motors must have taken a lesson from the Titanic when it came to building oil pans. We scraped and slid our way to the dunes where Daddy "put the peddle to the metal," and ignoring Mother's screams, gunned the poor little Buick to relative freedom on a road which actually was traversed once in a while.

Back at the post, we had a tub of smelly fish to scale and clean, an activity my father believed every proper young lady and future homemaker should master. Because Daddy was Daddy, I went along with his philosophy but have never cleaned or scaled another fish since about 1951. That is because......If you are not an Arizona history buff you can stop reading here.

That year I arrived home to find Daddy quite excited about a government project to enlarge our beloved fishing hole. A government bigwig had come

Navajo workers building a stone wall as part of a dam on Kaibito Creek (also called Big Wash and Kaibito Wash) 3 miles south of Kaibeto Trading Post, which Elizabeth Anne and her father visited in early summer "about 1951". A map shows the dam was at a narrow part of the stream valley, upstream from which was a large drainage area that would have been captured by the dam, said by her father to have created a lake at least 70 feet deep and a mile long (3 miles on one map). In the fall of 1952, however, the dam was washed away in an abnormally wet year. Had the dam been built a year or more later it might have served a long time providing fish and fishing for the traders and Natives and water for their sheep.

across our little lake and determined that by diverting nearby Kaibeto Wash into it, a very long waterway would magically appear. Daddy drove me to the construction site of the new dam where a large group of Navajo men were enjoying the rare opportunity of gainful employment and happily anticipating the creation of a huge source of precious water.

Daddy should have known, I should have known, and even those workers should have known what was going to happen. That year's rainy season was one of the most prolific ever experienced in that area. When Kaibeto Wash completed its cycle not a trace of Frenchman's Lake or the new dam could be found. Few people ever knew of Frenchman Lake's existence, but it did play a part in the Navajo Nation's early economy and nomadic culture. Thus, I felt the need to record its brief and tragic history. I doubt that anyone else ever will.

[**Editor's Note:** Adding to this history from family notes, Elizabeth Anne reports two lakes--Frenchman's Lake was 15 miles northeast of Kaibeto Trading Post at a site that is now called Dejolie Tank. This lake was on a tributary of Kaibito Creek (also called Kaibito Wash) and dated perhaps from CCC days. The second lake was said by her father to be 3 miles south of the trading post, behind a dam that was under construction up Kaibito Creek about 1951, and when completed he said it backed water up at least a mile. This period was about the time Elizabeth Anne reports prolific rain and the washing away of the newly-finished dam on Kaibito Creek and perhaps also the original and/or a new dam at Frenchman's Lake on the Kaibito Creek tributary, conceivably due to extra water being diverted into it from Kaibito Creek. And so fishing was over, as was the scaling of fish.]

Watermelons! One of the best parts of a trading post summer was the watermelon truck. The Hopi tribe grew many varieties of fruit in impossibly dry and sandy gardens, but their watermelons were the sweetest of all their produce. We never knew when Mark (can't recall his last name) was going to come rumbling up the road with a truck load of these luscious offerings, but there was always enough cash on hand to pay his asking price. By the time the truck was unloaded, Kaibeto's population had increased by at least a hundred.

We sold the melons whole or cut in half, but few survived to be carried to pickup or wagon. Instead, time stopped as, with juices running down chins and dripping off elbows, we all slurped and chewed down to the last suggestion of pink by the rind.

Daddy sliced his piece in a big round right out of the middle, added salt (yuk), then used his pocketknife to snare each bite. He would hand me a huge wedge which I ate without benefit of utensils while sitting atop the fence with everyone else who could crowd into the shade provided by our big cotton wood trees. We may have been a group divided by language and culture, but on watermelon day we were supremely united by taste buds and flavor. Mother, who always got sick when she ate watermelon, was left alone to tend the store and so missed this wonderful communion of like souls. I don't think she ever had any customers.

Many mornings Mother and I woke to a rousing chorus of "And He walks with me and He talks with me" as Daddy's baritone belted out his favorite hymn during his pre-opening chores. It may have been the only hymn he knew by heart as I never heard him sing any other. The day after watermelon day we were always treated to a somewhat longer performance as he cleared up the carnage left from consuming a half ton of Hopi land's finest product. Even the wild donkeys which feasted on the rinds during the night couldn't completely clear the evidence of our gluttony.

Another reason Daddy's arrival for his breakfast of bacon, two fried eggs, toast and a bowl of oatmeal was delayed might be that he was checking on several potential employees. Every trading post was a haven for stray cats and ours was no exception. They were welcome but expected to earn their keep. Once a litter of kittens was about half grown, the mother cat always seemed to disappear. Daddy would carefully feed the kittens a mixture of half canned milk and water until he deemed them ready for employment.

One feature of the warehouse was a platform where twenty-five and fifty pound sacks of flour were stacked to the ceiling. This arrangement enabled both cats and mice to scurry over the flour sacks and reach the plywood floor of the attic which stretched over both store and living quarters. This attic floor was also our ceiling; thus all the athletic competition was highly audible to occupants underneath. The scramble of tiny mice feet followed by the much longer and louder strides of flying feline was a nightly choreography which usually began about the time Mother was ready for bed. Her solution was to give the living room ceiling a few good whacks with a broom handle and yell "Quiet" at the top of her lungs. This never slowed the combatants at all but provided fine entertainment for a little girl who never liked going to bed early and was always awake for the performance.

After mastering the cash drawer, I received a new responsibility and promotion to "cigarette girl." Almost all Navajo men smoked, but I never saw even one lady with a cigarette. Even as a very small girl I could reach the cigarette display which was a glass mini display case composed of four shelves about twelve inches deep. I loved keeping it stocked and tidy. Bottom shelf was for chewing tobacco and Bull Durham. Other shelves held Lucky Strikes, Camels, Kools, and Phillip Morris all of which sold for fifteen cents a pack. During winter when the door had to be closed, we worked in a blue haze of smoke from dawn to dusk. Ash trays were not provided and at closing Mother checked the entire bull pen for smoldering cigarettes and usually found at least one.

Daddy was also a smoker, but his favorite smoke was a roll-your- own effort which seldom succeeded. After supper, he would retire to his chair by the big radio in the corner of the living room and begin the arduous task of manufacturing his smoke. He held the cigarette paper in one hand while with the other he attempted to extract just the right amount of tobacco. Once that was accomplished, for the duration of this delicate business, the strings on the little tobacco pouch were held between his teeth. The little paper was carefully folded around the tobacco, most of which had fallen out by now, then twisted and licked along the side. Since he was still holding those strings between his teeth, this was an almost impossible feat. He usually ended up with something about the size and shape of a small withered green bean. Nine times out of ten when he applied the match the whole cigarette went up in flames. He never got any better at this and used to try to convince Mother that the spilled tobacco was good for the little Navajo rug in front of his chair. One of my small girl housekeeping chores was to carefully fold that little rug around the tobacco each morning, carry it outside and give it a good shake. I am looking at that rug right now and it really is in good shape for an eighty some year old. Maybe Daddy was right!

Nothing is more crucial to the life of a trading post than its water supply, and ours was no exception. Atop our supporting mesa was a huge (I am guessing 10,000 gallon) water tank. It was buried right up to its cement top, and I wish I knew how it got there. No one else seemed to know either, so perhaps we can again blame those CCC fellows and their many untold accomplishments.

Our water actually came from a spring which was located about a half mile down the "little wash." This spring had a small opening where one could peek into its mysterious depths. The smell of earth and sounds of drippings enticed me to sit for long periods of time trying to imagine how far back the spring reached and what really went on in there. My imagination did not include wondering how that water made its way up to the humongous tank. We will deal with that tomorrow--and maybe the day after. Right now we will get back to the big tank on the mesa.

Since reaching the "bacterial age" with all its cautions and fears, I have often wondered about the purity of our water supply. The tank top did have a round loose-fitting lid, much like a manhole cover, which was secured by a padlock. Periodically, Daddy would unlock the cover and shine a flashlight into the depths. If he ever saw anything other than water down there, it wasn't mentioned. He never offered to share his findings with me. With that cover not being tightly sealed and given the frequency of dust storms in the area, a bottom layer of sand and a few small insects would have been a sure thing. Since the spring also had an opening, it is not only possible but quite probable that a small animal occasionally fell in and drowned. What came out of our faucet, however, was always clear and refreshing and we drank with great appreciation. With today's standards for water purity, it is amazing that all three of us lived into our eighties and one of us is still here to tell the tale. If any of our visiting relatives is reading this, it may be that you can thank your longevity on the immunity you acquired from drinking Kaibeto water during your visits.

The last time I visited Kaibeto, the only structure still standing was the pump house. That seemed most fitting as that little building was the heart of our tiny settlement. Constructed of the same rock and mortar materials as the old government school, it was probably part of the same government or CCC project. Inside, mounted on a cement block, was a two by four foot hunk of mysterious metal. Little room was left for the person who had to crank, cajole, and swear at this collection of pulleys, wheels and dip sticks until it came to life. On the rare occasion when Daddy allowed me to accompany him when it was his turn to start the pump, I had to press myself against the wall to keep out of his way.

About twice a week, depending on the current population, the pump had to be pampered, primed, and persuaded to start. First the lone spark plug was removed, scraped with the pocketknife, and carefully replaced. A gallon of gasoline was poured into one orifice and a liberal dose of motor oil into another. Then began the cranking process which was reminiscent of starting a Ford Model T. Daddy always worked up a good sweat at this point and although not given to colorful language, treated my small ears to some interesting mumblings as he repeatedly plucked his "farmer Brown" hankie from his overall pocket and wiped his streaming brow. Finally, the cursed machine would emit a feeble cough which progressed to a steady roar. The little room then filled with smoke so pungent we inhaled the equivalent of ten years of urban living. Now that we finally have it started, we will let it run for a while. Tomorrow we may figure out how all this resulted in a nice glass of cold water when we got home.

Yesterday we were in the pump house, smoke pouring out its door and one tiny window. The pump had done its usual reluctant start and Daddy had not had a heart attack from all his exertions in making it come to life. We lingered until the smoke dissipated a bit and the roar of the pump echoed from every rock and crevice in our little valley. We had learned from experience that if we left too soon, the pump, having a mind of its own, would stop running as we neared the halfway point on our walk back. But this was not just any walk. Outside the pump house there was an overflow pipe which produced sufficient moisture in drips and drabs to create a large area of dampness. This gave spawn to a luxuriant cottonwood tree and also a crop of prize-winning tumble weeds.

Agnes Begay, one of the employees at the day school, noticed this unusual display of vegetation, deftly ousted the weeds, and planted what was probably the only successful victory garden on the entire reservation. If it was summer and Agnes was tending her garden, we were treated to a freshly pulled carrot or radish or even a tomato, all properly wiped clean on her voluminous skirt. We munched these on the way home while Daddy gave me careful instructions on my duties for the remainder of the afternoon. I was to stay outside and listen for the pump to begin running unevenly or come to a stop. He was to be notified at once as there were various recoverings and recappings which needed to be performed while the pump was still warm. This generally occurred in about three hours. I usually forgot and it was Mother's sharp ears that picked up the death throes of the monster in the pump house. My parent's instructions were probably an agreed upon three-hour break from having me underfoot in the trading post.

Yesterday I said we would figure out how all this spring/ pump/ tank/ business resulted in our water supply. I haven't a clue. Somehow that pump sucked the water out of the spring and chased it up that high mesa and into that tank. I do know that gravity then brought it down to us.

We have mentioned the term "bull pen" before, but I will remind you that back in those bygone days it was the central part of every trading post. I have always felt it was a rather derogatory term since it was literally a pen from whence all aspects of trading took place. Customers were confined to the pen and separated from the trader and all his goods There was a four-foot-wide counter surrounding the bull pen and a railing about eighteen inches high overlooking that. It was definitely a formidable barrier. Since the Navajo way is to adjust to surroundings rather than becoming frustrated by them, the railing soon enabled anyone so inclined to lean in total comfort and set his own pace for shopping, pawning, rug selling or just having a chat with the trader.

Kaibeto's bull pen had a dark wooden slab floor, oiled so often by my diligent father that it appeared to be solid. This oiling was necessary to keep the dust at bay, but even so daily sweeping was necessary. During winter there was a wood burning stove, not the potbellied variety shown in most pictures, but an oblong affair with two round openings which required a constant supply of small logs. The counter blocked any heat circulation, so those of us in back suffered from chilled feet and legs while bull pen occupants were usually wiping sweaty brows.

Another reason the floor had to be frequently oiled was the problem of tobacco juice. Many Navajo men were fond of the plug of raw tobacco popular in those times. Not all of them felt it necessary to do their spitting in a "Daddy approved" manner. A cardboard sign by the door read, "Do not spit on stove, floor or wall! Spit outside!" Unfortunately, in those early days, only about one in ten Navajo men could read English, so the sign was largely ignored. If a fellow did take the time to open the door and aim a squirt outward, it always landed on the cement steps to be tracked in by the next customer. If this makes the Navajo sound like extremely unsanitary people, we must remember that all hogans had dirt floors. Thus, a new floor was possible every morning and from the number of brooms we sold I am almost certain that was the case. Tomorrow more bull pen activities. It was a busy place.

When an entire family made the trip from hogan to trading post the bull pen soon became a hub of domestic activity. The youngest family member, still in a cradle board, usually arrived in need of lunch and was tended to immediately. It never occurred to a Navajo mother to debate whether breast feeding in public was permissible. If baby was hungry, baby was fed. This was accomplished with absolute modesty as traditional Navajo blouse/tops

Interior of the trading post, referred to as the "bull pen".

were the perfect cover up. Nothing other than the back of the infant's head was ever seen.

While mom deposited herself in an out of the way corner and provided that meal, dad was occupied with selecting the adult luncheon fare. This was carefully done one item at a time either by calling out the Navajo name of the desired product or by simply "lip pointing" to it on the shelf. Each item was paid for separately either by tendering cash or having it written in the credit ledger. A large can of sliced peaches, at least two cans of Vienna sausages, a box of saltine crackers and perhaps even a small can of whole tomatoes and a candy bar or two completed most menus. Other than a little help from the crackers, all this became "finger food" and was consumed without utensils. Toddlers happily held a peach slice in one hand and a sausage in the other, all the while smearing the juices over the bull pen wall.

All of us who have raised children know that mealtime is usually followed by potty time, and it was no different in this setting. Most often the little ones made it out the door in good time, but once in a while there was an accident which illustrated the Navajo's ingenious approach to potty training. Little girls wore a very full skirt and no undies and were taught to twirl around a time or two so as not to soil the pretty skirt. A boy simply wore pants which had been split open at the crotch. It was almost always a little boy who did not quite make it through the door. Mother kept a supply of rags for those occasions. At this point you are probably thinking, "How terrible". But please

Elizabeth Anne is giving her dog "Lollypop the Terrible" a bath in a tub, the same tub and same way the family did their weekly laundry until Elizabeth Anne's freshman year in high school when electricity allowed a washing machine. Before that, evening lighting was with kerosene lamps and the refrigerator used that fuel, too.

think again. If you had a couple of toddlers, no washing machine and thirty gallons of water to last for a week, what would you do? After six months or so of these homely activities, the bull pen wall was beyond description. Of course Daddy had a solution. I will let you guess until tomorrow how he solved the problem.

While Mother was the "Queen of Clean" behind the counter, it was Daddy's sole responsibility to keep the bull pen wall and floor in some semblance of sanitation. His solution to this and a host of other troublesome situations was a good thick coat of paint. Most Navajos traveled in open buckboard wagons which, like Mr. Ford's flivver, came in any color as long as you wanted black. In the case of wagons, the choice was green, and Daddy kept a good supply of wagon paint on hand. Aptly named "wagon green," it was a big seller because it kept some of the sandstorm damage at bay. It also covered a multitude of sins as far as the bull pen was concerned. A liberal coat was applied to that area at least once every six months.

When the supply truck arrived, any new paint was stored behind what was already on hand. Thus, when a dozen cans of "Pansy Pink" paint arrived, no one spied the difference. This might have been because the warehouse had only two very small dirt encrusted windows. Due to their placement along the ceiling, these windows had never been washed. Paint sales must have been a bit slow for a while, for by the time Daddy noticed the error, it was long past the point of no return.

As I have mentioned before, the Navajo culture believes in adjusting oneself to the circumstances instead of trying to fight against them. Scratch that when it came to painting a wagon pansy pink. It was wagon green or nothing. Thus, for about four years Kaibeto Trading Post was adorned with pink counters, pink railing, and bullpen. I still don't know if it was his masculinity or his wife which kept Daddy from painting the shelves and even the front door pink. Since the railings and the counter didn't get as dirty as the bull pen walls, they were not painted as frequently. Finally, when Daddy had finished his latest coating of pansy pink on the counters and rails and reached for what he thought was going to be the last can of that color, he found himself holding a can of something called "lime green." For about a year we had lime green bullpen augmented by pansy pink counter and railing. The Navajos never seemed to notice our merry color scheme, but there were some traders and Bureau of Indian Affairs employees in the area who had a good laugh.

I have already mentioned Lollypop the Terrible, my constant companion from earliest childhood. During any brief time she was not with me her favorite activity was to lunge beside our wire fence while snarling and snapping at anything that walked on two or four legs. I will never forget the day she came limping toward me with a four-inch flap of skin hanging down so far she was stepping on it, enlarging the gash with every step. Young as I was, I knew my beloved dog was going to die and I can still hear my own screams which were so loud that Mr. Mobly, the current day school teacher, reached the scene before either of my parents. That turned out to be a day that God looked with favor on a little girl who loved her dog more than anything.

Mr. Mobly acknowledged that he had been a conscientious objector during the war. I think that meant that while he would never harm another human being, he was not averse to repairing those who were not in agreement with him. Daddy was a doctor's eldest son and sometimes regaled us with stories of holding the lantern while his father delivered babies, amputated limbs, and performed other dangerous procedures. With all this medical experience between them, these two decided to try to put Lollypop back together again. Commandeering Mother's built-in pie crust rolling board for an operating table, Mr. Mobly sewed while Daddy held the patient down and poured copious amounts of mercurochrome.

I didn't see this of course, as Mother, who was just sure the patient would not survive the surgery, dragged me down to the store to await the outcome. We heard only one small yelp which made us believe the worst. It seemed forever before I was called to visit Lolly in her doll bed, her middle wrapped snugly in one of Mother's best tea towels. She was very quiet, so I sat down to wait for her to die. Mother made me a makeshift bed beside the doll bed. Next morning Daddy and Mr. Mobly changed the bandage and found very little bleeding. Even so Mother had to sacrifice another pristine tea towel.

After that, Mother took a pair of pliers and spent a couple of hours inspecting every inch of fencing until she found the strand which had come loose and still held a little piece of Lolly. It was, of course, too late to include that in the surgical expertise, so Lolly always had a small pucker in her side. Within two weeks Lolly was back to her pell-mell lunges down the fence line, but there was never any more bloodletting.

Maybe there should be a PS to this one. Neither Daddy nor Mr. Mobly were averse to a little "nip" now and then. How they managed to sedate that feisty little Chihuahua and stitch her with what appeared to be almost no pain has always made me wonder? Anyone have any idea on how they might have administered a dram or two of Jack Daniels?

We always had a Christmas tree, and we always had a Scrooge. Unfortunately, "Scrooge" was the one who had to provide the tree and that was no small task. Mother had a phenomenal collection of Christmas ornaments, each of which had to be carefully unwrapped from its cotton batting and hung where it would show to its best advantage. The process took at least two days and required a tree that came within an inch of the ceiling. The area around Kaibeto was well populated with scrub cedar, scrub being the operative word. Due to the erratic weather patterns of that area, most trees were stunted and gnarled. Daddy had to hunt long and hard to find a suitable specimen, figure out a way to attach it to our poor little Buick, get it home, drag it through a couple of skinny doors and then fashion a stand which would accommodate what was always an extreme case of lopsidedness. All this effort was punctuated by an amazing amount of groaning and griping, and I suspect a nip or two from the Jack Daniels side of the family. Why anyone would want to go to this much trouble to bring a tree inside and put a bunch of bangles on it, was more than he could see.

Somewhere along the way, things became easier when Daddy discovered that a block of sheep salt which weighed about twenty-five pounds made an excellent tree stand. He then screwed two big hooks into the wall behind the tree, looped a long piece of baling wire around its trunk and attached the wire ends to each hook. This did not do much for the ambiance of our Yuletide setting, but it made sure nothing short of Santa's sleigh and all eight reindeer would cause that tree to topple. Mother always tried to wait for my return from school to decorate, and when we finished, even though we had no electricity for lights, it was always beautiful. Then "Scrooge" spent the next ten days bringing every Navajo from Cow Springs to Shonto up into our living room to view our handiwork.

Most old timers like me would be able to remember the exact year of the BIG SNOW, but the best I can say Is that I think it took place around the time I was in 4th grade, maybe 1946. We had a very white Christmas that year with snow piled right up to the post roof and telephone lines frozen and snarled.

It came time for me to go back to school. After augmenting his "survival kit" with a few more cans of Vienna Sausage and some oranges, Daddy and I set off very early one morning. It was slow going as tire chains were necessary to get us as far as Tonalea. While he removed the chains it began snowing again. Bathroom break at Grey Mountain while Daddy chained up again and didn't listen to the advice of friends who said we were not going to make it. On we went until it became obvious we were the only vehicle on the road. The little Buick's ability as a snowplow was severely limited. Managing to turn around, we slipped and slid our way back to Cameron where I spent the evening being spoiled by all the adults and daddy spent the evening worrying about Mother worrying about him not getting back that evening.

After adding even more emergency supplies to the survival kit, we set off again the next morning driving through a world of glittering pine trees and snow piled high as ten feet on either side of the road. Winslow didn't have so much as a flake of snow, but the sky was dark and threatening, and Daddy practically threw me and my belongings in the house before departing. I remember him telling Aunt Zada, "Sorry to use the can and run, but the only chance I have of getting home tonight is if I leave NOW!" We had no way of knowing if he reached Kaibeto safely that evening, but I knew Daddy and his beloved little car, and all those Vienna Sausages would eventually prevail. The entire Kaibeto Plateau was paralyzed for nearly three weeks during that time and the occupants survived only because an airlift was organized to drop hay, cases of canned goods, bags of flour (which almost always burst and were useless) and other necessities to the stricken area.

Ah, but there is more to this story. The media back then consisted only of radio reports, and true to its culture it reported only the most worrisome facts. Every hour on the hour we could hear about how no one knew if the people of Kaibeto were alive or dead. We had no reason for concern as one of the airlift pilots knew my aunt was the sister of the Kaibeto trader. He kindly took the time to call and let us know that as he flew over the trading post both the trader and his wife and quite a few other people were standing out front waving up at him. Somehow that happy fact never made the news which would have killed the story and made it necessary to find something else for us all to worry over.

I don't know when Spam made its appearance on our shelves, but it was definitely not a big seller for the Navajos. Vienna Sausages were one of our biggest sellers, and once in a while Armour Corned Beef made its way to the bullpen luncheon buffet. Thus, the unsold Spam became a regular on our personal dinner menu. Mother could probably have edited a cookbook on different ways to make the stuff edible. She did something with sugar and cinnamon that was pretty tasty, but her effort to flavor canned green beans with onions and Spam was dismal.

Traders ate pretty much what was on their shelves and after a twelve-hour day looking at all those cans a lot of them "drank" their first and maybe even their second course before facing what was on their plate. Mother made some sort of white cream sauce with canned milk and flour and then added a can of green peas, or tuna, or corn. It was not all that bad and having the word "creamed" in front of the can of the day made us feel a bit elegant.

We sold bacon which we cut from huge slabs, and every breakfast was nearly the same. We sat down to bacon, fried eggs, luscious pancakes with melted butter added to the batter and more butter poured over them as they came off the griddle. A big bowl of oatmeal topped with sugar and canned milk rounded out that important first meal of the day. The oatmeal pan, its contents congealed and opaque, remained on the back of the behemoth wood stove the entire day. Any leftovers from lunch or supper were deposited therein and presented to the two dogs. They deemed the whole mess so delicious we had to stand back for fear of being run over before their dishes hit the floor.

Like most cooks of her day, Mother had a grease can with a strainer inside which culled out the little burned pieces of bacon and other debris. Due to generous additions from the grease can, her pinto beans were legendary and probably the cause of a more than a few heart attacks. It makes my mouth water just to write about them. She served the daily oatmeal for no other reason than because it stuck to one's ribs and had no idea it was probably counteracting all the cholesterol in most everything else we consumed. As I have mentioned before, both of my parents lived to be 82. The dogs lived to be at least a hundred in dog years. I don't know how many of my 84 years I can attribute to all that oatmeal, but I do know I am still carrying around a few extra pounds courtesy of the grease can.

At least three times a week during winter Mother and I woke to the clanging and scraping of Daddy removing ash from the two wood burning stoves. He then inserted a small amount of bark and kindling which was topped by several crumpled pages of an expired "Monkey Wards" catalog. A half a cup or so of kerosene and some larger sticks of wood were added to the pyre and then came the big moment. Standing at least three feet back, Daddy struck a match and threw it in the stove with one hand while grabbing the stove door with the other and shutting it with lightning speed. I never saw him singe so much as an eyebrow with this death defying pyrotechnic, and he always beat the resulting "Whooooosh" from inside the stove by a micro-second. He used the same technique on the stove in the bull pen, and it is a wonder that our trading post was one of the few which never had a major fire.

The behemoth stove in the kitchen was a little trickier since it had to be serviced through the little round openings on its top. It required more kindling and more catalog and only a drop of kerosene. By the time Mother was up she was then able to add the required pieces of regular size wood without becoming a human torch. The living room stove stood in front of a cement block fireplace of which I have only the vaguest memory. I do remember having my bath in a big round tin tub placed in front of that fire-place. I also recall that one evening when the tub was a bit closer to the fire than usual, I leaned back against the side of the tub nearest the fireplace. Next thing my parents knew they had a screaming wet and naked four-year-old running around the living room. I was a "screamer" at the least provocation, so I didn't get much sympathy until I heard Daddy say. "Julia, you had better look at this". Of course, I couldn't see what sort of stripe I had acquired, but it must have been pretty vivid for it was one of the few times Mother didn't think that Vicks was a cure all, nor did Daddy proffer his miracle cure of Sloan's liniment. I can't recall what, if anything, was applied to ease my pain, but I am sure I played it to the hilt.

Trading post living quarters showing screened porch at left, where Elizabeth Anne and her mother Julia awakened one morning to snow that had blown in on their blankets.

Frenchman's Lake was a desert lake behind a dam on a tributary to Kaibito Creek. This photograph is undated but a similar one is from the late 1940s. The dam itself may date from a CCC project, then another project in the 1950s that intended to enlarge the lake and bring water to it from Kaibito Creek. All this has since been washed away, probably during an extreme rainy period in 1952, especially in late September when 3 1/2 inches of rain fell in 3 days in a desert climate that normally gets barely 6 inches per year. The lake was at or near Dejolie Tank, shown on modern maps, and aerial photographs show a dam breached by the tributary just downstream from Dejolie Tank.

The Hitching Post beside the trading post, Navajo man with sidearm.

LEFT: Ralph Jones, WWI uniform. Ralph's military background may have made him more understanding of the plight of Navajo servicemen when they attempted readjustment to reservation life. **RIGHT:** Trader Ralph with snow around the post, a sight not uncommon in the Kaibito region, which is at an altitude of 5,800 feet, high desert. Occasionally major storms would strand Natives in their dispersed homesites, at times requiring air drops of supplies. – *circa 1946*

Julia Jones leads a horse tour of the trading post area, leaving behind Elizabeth Anne, who loved horses but not riding them. (Julia is in plaid shirt.)

BELOW: Aunt Zada Jones Purdy "horse" with young Elizabeth Anne astride, along with Zada's daughters – Rosemary and Suzanne, with whom Elizabeth Anne lived later when attending Winslow schools. Zada at a time was Elizabeth Anne's school teacher, too, and assisted at the trading post during times of family emergencies.

LEFT: Elizabeth Anne in high school, *circa 1952.*
BOTTOM: Elizabeth Anne with one of her many dolls, about age 3.

Halo, everybody. Halo! Halo is the shampoo that "glorifies" your hair. I am not sure that glorifies is the correct word. No matter, even though that marvelous shampoo hit the shelves sometime during my preteens (I think), Mother and I had something better. Down through the years, probably no part of man's grooming process has evolved as much as hair washing. When I was young, hair was washed every two weeks whether it needed it or not. No one ever thought of showering and washing hair at the same time. In fact, hardly anyone ever thought of showering. Shampooing consisted of wetting the hair in a basin, applying shampoo, rinsing, and then doing the whole thing over again, plus one more rinse. You were never to go outside until your hair was completely dry or you would catch your death of cold. Going to bed before hair was dry would bring the same fate. If you were a lady, you were advised to never wash your hair during "that time of the month." The reason for this edict was never explained but was taken very seriously.

While Mother and I kept most of these superstitions, our shampoo was a bit different. Either Agnes Begay or her sister Ada would bring us the roots of a yucca plant, which we then pounded and flattened as much as possible. When dipped in a basin of warm water, the most glorious and fragrant suds exploded from those roots. From there, the process was pretty much the same. The only difference was our hair was much softer and shinier than when we used regular shampoo. The slight problem of a few little twigs and pieces of bark that needed to be removed during the drying process was dealt with easily. Cream rinse was unheard of back then, so shampooing always involved a certain amount of pain as tangles and snarls were removed. Not so with this Navajo shampoo. Sticks and snarls fell out as if by magic. This was a very good thing as Mother always used shampoo time to comb through my hair with one of those tiny toothed little "fine combs" to make sure nothing living had taken up residence in my thick mop of hair.

As traders, we may have had primitive bathing and cooking facilities, but I am sure our media center was state of the art. Given enough bailing wire, my father could solve most any problem, and he had a yen to listen to the radio. Our first radio, which I remember mostly for its bursts of static was the size of a small refrigerator. It stood in the corner of the living room and eventually served as a platform for its replacement. The next radio, which now resides in a family cabin near Payson, was about one fourth that size but required a battery that today would provide sufficient power for a small city. Tubes as large as today's light bulbs completed its inward parts. Along with

Trader Ralph Jones posing at a road sign telling how far it is to go on dirt/sand or rock roads like the one under the Buick, his favorite car.

a wicked looking handgun, Daddy kept the extra battery and tubes hidden inside the first radio. And yes, the gun was loaded!

Now the challenge was to find a way to get some sort of reception. Bailing wire firmly attached to the radio, poked through the nearest window, then wound around the lightning rod by the doghouse brought only mediocre results. Daddy kept going until the wire was twisted onto the barbed wires of the back yard fence. That night we enjoyed "Your Hit Parade" and "Grand Ole Opry." Daddy felt there had to be more, and before we knew it he had strung his (now knotted together many times) pieces of wire to the top of the mesa. It worked! We never missed any of the popular radio programs and often took our dinner plates into the living room to join with "Great Gildersleeve" or "The Red Skeleton Show" (how I loved it when Red played the part of the "mean little kid"), "The Shadow," "Inner Sanctum," and "The Whistler." This all sent Mother off to bed early, telling Daddy he would have to be the one who got up with me when I had bad dreams. I never did have any nightmares, probably because I stuffed my fingers in my ears during the really scary parts.

Jack Benny was our favorite, especially enjoyable along with the sound effects when he entered his money vault. The biggest moment of our week, however, was always when Fibber McGee opened his hall closet, and every object one's mind could possibly conjure up came tumbling out.

Oh right--you are wondering about the gun. We will talk more about that tomorrow.

Yesterday I left you wondering why my father would leave a loaded handgun hidden away in a spot so easily reached by his priceless only child. That is rather the way things were back in those days. I always knew the gun was there and it never occurred to me to touch it or investigate it in any way. By the time grandchildren came along, Daddy had completely changed his outlook on this practice. Once he became a grandfather, the gun and its ammunition were so widely separated that the bad guy would have been able to walk out with everything in the house, including my mother, before Daddy would have been able to get the weapon ready to fire.

The reason for having a gun at a trading post was grim and grisly, and I suspect most traders had a much larger arsenal than Daddy's little radio shelf arrangement. Gladstone Richardson, a member of one of the earliest trading families, wrote an excellent account of very early trading posts. According to him, many of those first posts and their proprietors met terrible fates. By the time we came along, the Arizona Territory was a much more civilized and calm area, but the stories lingered on. Daddy's little radio corner was strategically chosen so that he had a "bead" on any bad guys who might show up during the time the store was closed. Thankfully nothing like that ever happened.

Without meaning to, Daddy did once come close to shooting someone. We sold .22 rifles which came in wooden crates and needed some assembly. I wasn't there for this tale, but Mother retold it so often it has become real in my mind. We had visitors, I think maybe one of my uncles or older cousins and they were watching Daddy assemble one of the rifles. His Army experience had taught Daddy that part of this chore was to put plenty of spit and polish on the gun before displaying it. Daddy was rubbing with great vigor, turning the gun every which way when the visiting family member admonished him not to be pointing it so recklessly. Daddy told him there was no danger as he had just put the gun together and there was no way it could be holding a bullet. To demonstrate, Daddy pointed the gun toward the floor, pulled the trigger and BLAM! It was a great shot. It not only missed the observers but didn't even come close to Daddy's foot and left only a small hole in the wooden floor.

Bedbugs! When Gladwell Richardson, the author I mentioned a couple days ago, wrote about the early, early Kaibeto, he devoted more space to these little devils than most anything else. When my parents moved to Kaibeto they found the entire place infested with a virulent variety of Chinese bedbug which supposedly had been dropped off by a missionary who had recently returned from China. During the remodel, both my parents and the construction workers placed the legs of their sleeping cots in small cans of kerosene. This worked well as far as keeping the nasty creatures from climbing onto the bed from the floor. There was no deterrent that prevented them from climbing the wall and then coasting down on an unsuspecting sleeper. Being bitten by one of these dive bombers produced huge painful welts which did not disappear for days. It was said that a small child could die from just a few bites.

When Mr. Richardson and his brother returned to Inscription House Trading Post after helping get things ready for business at Kaibeto, his sister-in-law required them to give her every stitch of their clothing to be boiled. Knowing Susie, she probably also laced the tub with a generous dose of lye. Hopefully they had sufficient wardrobe to change into other clothes.

By the time I was born, the bedbug population was on the wane. Mother had that effect on anything that crossed her path uninvited. But, taking no chances, she ordered a special baby crib from somewhere in New York. I still can remember that crib because it was large enough for me to sleep in until I was at least five. Instead of slats, it had rectangular areas about two feet wide and one foot high on each side and every area which wasn't wood was screen. When in place, the top bent over and came to a peak. Absolutely no foreign critter could breech that little fortress. It also served to keep sweet little me from roaming about after candles and lanterns were extinguished.

A Father's Day tribute to a good Navajo trader: Flagstaff, which was 125 miles away was a sort of home base for trading posts, and Daddy usually had business there at least every six weeks. Nothing seemed right when Daddy wasn't at the trading post, and I don't think I ever let Mother out of my sight on those days. It would always be dark before we saw the headlights and heard the distinct rattle of the little Buick creeping back down the hill. Both of us sighing in relief, we hurried to hoist the warehouse door. Soon as Daddy emerged, he always kissed Mother right on the lips and me on the top of my head. He never failed to bring both of us a little gift and when he could find them, always had bananas for both of us.

Next morning always found Daddy's suit pants with suspenders still attached hung over the corner of the living room door and his jacket suspended from the knob. He knew this annoyed the tar out of Mother who would mumble about him not knowing there was a perfectly good closet three feet away. I think he had that same grey suit for at least twenty years. He had courtly manners when required, but the conventions of the times were never a worry.

During the war when the little Buick suffered an unfortunate meeting with a cow (they both survived), Daddy pounded out the dent, painted over it with regular house paint, and showed no embarrassment at the less than beautiful results. Forty-six years old when I was born, he never expected to have grandchildren. Our youngest was twelve when Daddy died, and I know those years of grandparenting were his happiest. No grandfather was ever more proud or indulgent. Each of our children have a priceless store of memories from time spent with my parents after they retired in Camp Verde. That is where I saw him last. A week later he was gone.

Most of you don't believe in such things, and I am not sure I do, but I think Daddy had one more thing he intended to do. He firmly believed that all kids, especially boys, should have a dog. We had cats when our kids were young, but really hadn't given any thought to a dog. Within a few days of Daddy's death, a cute little mutt followed our son home from school (at least that is the story I have been told). Our son named him Muttlee and he was a crazy, funny, loyal and loving creature who saw us through many a tough day. Did the ever-indulgent grandpa make one last transaction before entering his eternal rest? You be the judge.

Tony Burns, this one is for you. Why don't all homes, buildings, structures of any sort have tin roofs? Today it is hot as blue blazes, and our AC hasn't shut down since early morning. I can't help but wonder if a nice, shiny galvanized tin roof might make a big difference. For all the hodgepodge of rooms that made up our trading post, one thing was constant. The entire structure was snugly covered in tin. It gleamed bright during the day and shone faintly when the moon was full. The heat reflected off it during the summer, so we never needed so much as a fan. During winter it could hold several inches of snow with no complaint. In nearly thirty years of occupancy, it never required one single repair. With all the grooves, the attached rain gutters filled instantly which made sure even the shortest shower filled our cistern to overflowing. And, oh--being anywhere inside the building during a rainstorm was sheer ecstasy. The sound effects, which might be compared to being inside a snare drum while a Sousa March is played, are like no other experience life has to offer. A hailstorm required fingers in ears but was still exhilarating.

After the disappointing collapse of our sand cave, my cousin Fay and I discovered how to walk on the roof. If we went early enough, we could wend our way to the spot where the big cottonwood trees covered the screened in porch. We had to watch the time because that saying about a cat on a hot tin roof has a great deal of validity. Beneath those thick leafy boughs it stayed cool all day.

From that lofty perch we could not only see most anything that was happening, but also hear everything the adults below us were discussing. I am sure they knew we were up there and probably loved it that we were trapped until the roof cooled off. We always took Nancy Drew and her chums with us along with a jar of peanut butter and a box of crackers. The surly chihuahua liked it up there too, so my grandmother's ankles were safe for a few hours. Mother did mention once that she was afraid we might fall off, and I am surprised that we never did. At least we were not in danger of anything falling on us.

It was always easy to figure out who were the local "bootleggers." Large purchases of sugar and any sort of fruit in season, especially peaches or apricots, were the clue. Most of the Kaibeto folks stayed with the sheep industry and seemed to be teetotalers. But as my grandmother Jones would say, "Demon Rum always has to rear its ugly head."

As much as I roamed around the area I never ran across a still, so they must have been carefully hidden. We did hear a chilling story that once during the time my first husband Bob and I were running the store, he came so close to stumbling over a still that a few more steps and he would have been shot. There is probably some truth in that because a few days later the bootlegger Dan (not his real name) did some serious shooting which left four dead and one wounded.

Bob had left for Flagstaff that afternoon so as to get an early start on business the next day, so it was a blessing I didn't get the news until the next morning. Our helper, now a young man named Gordon (name changed) arrived to tell me that "Dan had got him four women last night".

My reply was, "Dan is married. What is he doing messing around with all those women?"

"No. I mean he shot them."

No one had any idea where Dan might be. About midafternoon an FBI agent ambled in asking if we had seen Dan. When we replied in the negative, I was told that if Dan did show up I was to give him anything he asked for, including more ammunition.

I had read somewhere that FBI Agents can be a little dense, but if he thought a mother with three little kids on the premises was going to give a known killer more bullets, he needed a serious refresher course in public relations.

I had hidden all our ammunition and also enlisted the "cavalry" (a couple of Mormon missionaries) to keep the kids out of sight. Not long after that Bob arrived to swell our defenses. If I remember correctly, it was the Navajo police, not the FBI, who found Dan in a deserted hogan half dead from drinking Clorox. He survived and served many years in a prison in Oklahoma. Dan could write English, but his wife could not read it, so she had me read his letters to her. He often expressed regrets at what he did but never once explained why he did it.

Another source of water at the trading post was an old cistern which due to the slope of the tin roof, filled each time it rained. This tank was only a few feet from the back door, and its cement top must have been designed and installed by the same fellow who created our grotesque kitchen wall. To describe it as ugly would have been a compliment. The globular grey lump was topped by a wooden platform on which stood an old-fashioned hand pump. The water produced by this pump stank to high heaven and beyond but was highly prized by Mother for her house plants and garden flowers.

Of course the pump had to be primed and usually took three or four doses of regular water before it gushed forth its smelly payload. Getting one of those old pumps to work is one of life's sweetest experiences. Carting all those buckets of water to the marigolds and zinnias and young trees Mother loved so much wasn't nearly as much fun.

Whatever Mother planted and wherever she planted it, a seed always turned into a thriving plant. During summer our back yard was a riot of color. It had to have been the stinky water, as soil in our yard consisted of nothing more than plain old blow sand. Inside the house, every windowsill was graced with geraniums and violets all booming their hearts out no matter what season of the year. The summer before I left for college the old cistern evidently sprang a leak, for no matter how much rain fell or how vigorously we pumped, our buckets remained dry. Daddy removed the old pump but never got around to covering the resulting opening. Mother took to throwing all our empty tin cans in there, a very unlike Mother thing to do. Perhaps she was trying to get even because her flowers were never as beautiful after the old cistern gave up the ghost.

My cousin Ken loved to visit Kaibeto. Ken was one of those wonderful folks who knew no strangers. He spoke not a word of Navajo, but if he ran into Hosteen Tso who spoke no English, Ken soon knew how many children he had, and everything else important about him.

Ken also loved to explore the area on horseback, and he once persuaded me to accompany him on one of these excursions. I reluctantly agreed for I preferred to do my exploring with both feet on the ground instead of being seated on a thousand-pound animal I really didn't trust. Mother and I would occasionally hire a couple of Navajo ponies for a couple of hours, an endeavor Mother enjoyed far more than I. While I sat tense atop the beast hoping not to embarrass myself by grabbing the saddle horn, Mother rode beautifully as if welded to the pony.

Ken and I set off early one morning carrying the standard crackers and Vienna sausage lunch and a large canteen of water. My horse, like most Navajo ponies, was skinny and skittish and had absolutely no inner springs. By mid-day I was ready to go home, but Ken kept wanting to see what was over the next hill and the next and the next. Then he announced that we were lost. I told him all we had to do was climb out of the canyon we had just entered, look for Navajo Mountain and easily find our way back. This was true, but we had drifted so far north that many, many hills and valleys were between us and the trading post. It was hot and we had not rationed our water. I had never been that thirsty before and not knowing a lot about horses, I wondered if they would die of thirst along with me. At this point I wasn't too concerned about Ken's demise.

A trader family in "going to town" clothes for a 1940 trip to Flagstaff; Elizabeth Anne in cowboy boots.

Then, just as I caught a glimpse of cottonwood trees, the horse, as if sensing its misery was about to end, broke into a jagged trot and then a terrifying gallop. Someone had left the back gate open, and horse and I ended up by the kitchen door where the water hose lay coiled. I didn't even wait for the water to cool before I started taking great gulps and never has anything felt quite so wonderful. Thirst quenched, another great need arose. Abandoning the poor horse, I made a run for the bathroom only to find Mother ensconced therein. My desperate cry brought her out quickly. I did yell "horse" and pointed toward the back door as I made a record-breaking run toward another sort of saddle. Alas, I soon realized that eight hours in a horse saddle when you aren't used to it would mean that any body function in the foreseeable future was going to be accompanied by pain. That evening I ate my dinner off the fireplace mantle.

PS. Mother kindly tended to the horse for me. I suspect she also gave Ken a bit of a lecture.

It looks as if we may run out of trading post stories before we run out of pandemic. I do have one more horse story and a Christmas story. Mostly I am left with snippets of memories which I am not sure if I witnessed or have heard so many times I picture them in my mind.

One event I know I didn't witness was a plane crash my father wrote about in one of his letters. He was about a mile away at the sheep corral when an airplane flying directly overhead began to spit and sputter and then came spiraling down on the spot where he stood. He was sure there was no escaping and found himself running in circles trying to figure out if there was any way to survive. He said the noise became nearly unbearable right before a tremendous explosion and the plane was no longer to be seen. He stood there staring at a plume of dust which seemed to be more than a mile away and then noticed a little white "handkerchief" floating above all the dust. The handkerchief quickly turned into a parachute. The pilot, who was taking part in some sort of competition called the Bendix Race was uninjured and upset because he was just sure he was in the lead when his engine blew up.

Meanwhile, back at the trading post everyone was congratulating them-selves on being alive, for they had been sure the airplane was coming down on the roof. I guess if today's story has a moral, it is to relax the next time you think a plane is going to crash on you because it isn't very likely to happen. When I came home for Thanksgiving, Daddy took me to the crash site. For a very small plane, it made a very big hole but it was surprisingly intact.

It is hard to imagine what the Navajo of the thirties and forties thought of Christmas as I don't remember any of them being Christian. When I was in my early teens, there was a Navajo Reverend Bradley who held a sizable revival style camp meeting. Since food was provided, his service did draw a good crowd. If there were any converts, we didn't hear about it and he never returned.

What most traders did to celebrate the birth of Christ probably made a positive impression on their customers but fell far short of clarifying much. The Navajos called it "Kissmish" and it was a day they received a small gift for everyone in the family. We packaged these gifts in plain paper bags. I can remember filling at least two hundred. There was always an apple and an orange. Each adult male also received a package of cigarettes. Children were given Crakerjack and a handful of that wonderful hard candy so popular then. I wish I could remember what ladies received in addition to the fruit. I am thinking it was some sewing item such as needles which were highly prized. Everyone also received a candy bar, and each sack was topped off with a handful of peanuts in the shell. It all seems so little now, but when you are seven or eight and doling out that many candy bars or oranges it was huge. The hard candy was just tossed in with a scoop and of course stuck to everything else. No little plastic bags back then. I loved that candy and always had a tummy ache before we were finished.

Daddy's one concession to Christmas decorations in the trading post was a big cardboard Santa which he tacked up on the front of the pawn cupboard. No one ever commented or asked who that was supposed to be. The focus was always on the little sacks and their contents which were received as if we were giving away the Crown Jewels. This happy event always took place the day before Christmas as that was one day we did close. I am sure Daddy spent the day scraping candy and peanut shells off the floor. Mother cooked a dinner which could have fed fifteen for the three of us and sometimes the local district supervisor. The spoiled child never helped with any of this but spent the day playing with more toys than most children receive in a lifetime.

About seventy-five years ago, July the first saw many Kaibeto citizens setting off for the All Indian Powwow held in Flagstaff around Independence Day. Why leave so early? These hardy souls drove their wagons all that 125 miles. By this time in history, most Navajo people had some sort of motor conveyance, but there were still some who either by necessity or choice made the journey by horse and wagon. By July 3rd, Kaibeto was always a "ghost plateau" and we often closed the store and joined in the festivities. While we stayed at the ghost ridden Monte Vista Hotel, everyone else camped out around the fair grounds. Apache, Ute, Papago, Hopi, Navajo, and many other tribes all in native dress congregated happily together.

The biggest event was always the daily parade with each tribe showing off its unique dancing and cultural talents. Apache Devil Dancers, Hopi

Hoop Dancers, Navajo Yei (Spirit People), and the ladies (Papago?) carrying huge pottery jars atop their heads without ever reaching up to touch them always made my jaw drop. The next most important event was the rodeo which I hated, but which both Daddy and Mother enjoyed. I felt sorry for the poor little calves used in the roping contests and always secretly rooted for them. I had no sympathy when the human participant had to be carried off the grounds.

I, of course, could hardly wait for the Ferris wheel which Mother rode with me and the tiltawhirl which was Daddy's cross to bear until I became old enough to ride by myself. Mother got "seasick" just from watching us. There was also a lovely Merry-Go-Round which I could happily have ridden all day. Daddy always bought me cotton candy which I never had the nerve to tell him I didn't like. Not exactly Disneyland, but for its time considered one of the best traveling carnivals in the country. Finding someone to dog sit the vicious Lollypop was never easy, so we never stayed more than one day and night. Daddy always brought home enough fireworks to make poor Eddie Girl keep the wool pile trembling for several hours. Gradually the rest of Kaibeto's population drifted back, some a bit worse for wear due to rodeo activities. I always felt they deserved every bump and bruise.

Just spent several hours arguing with my iPad which didn't want to join the fun this afternoon. Actually, it had something to do with wifi which my husband figured out how to correct. All this made me realize I have completely forgotten how to cope with life without benefit of electricity. It also reminded me that although the time we have been remembering was between 1939 into the fifties, there are still some of the Navajo living almost exactly the way we did in those times.

At the trading post we used a Coleman lantern in the living room. Periodically, about once an hour I think, it had to be pumped when the light grew dimmer. Our other light was a single kerosene lamp which we carried from room to room as needed. For all the grown-up duties I was given, the lighting system was never included. I was a bit of a klutz and my parents probably figured, and rightly so, that I would set the house ablaze.

Trading was pretty much a sunup to sundown affair. Although we never opened at the crack of dawn, we did do business much later in summer than winter. Flashlights and batteries were big sellers. Both were expensive and we all used them sparingly as possible. The radio battery also was costly, and you didn't leave it on if you left the room for more than a minute. For a warm bath, we heated water in a bucket on the big wood stove in the kitchen, poured it in the galvanized tin tub and then diluted from the faucet until the temperature was tolerable. Before disrobing we hollered to anyone in the living room that it was bath time, so please stay out of the kitchen. A little more hot water was added for the next bather's turn. Summer was cold shower time, but at least you didn't have to share the water. Except during winter, when the ever-present teakettle furnished hot water to add to the cold in the basin, morning ablutions were quite refreshing and brisk. I think I will go outside and hug the hot water heater!

A couple weeks ago I wrote about Kaibeto being snowed in for several weeks. I guesstimated the winter of '48 or '49 and will stick by that date. Today we have a guest writer who lived through the event from the actual location. Unfortunately, he didn't give the exact date. Here is the letter he wrote to me back then:

"Dear Anne. We have been having quite a bit of excitement lately even if we are snowed in. The airlift made two direct hits on the buildings here with bales of hay. Only one Navajo was injured in that, but yesterday a case of milk got Joe Nez's wife in the head and decapitated her. She had a baby in her lap at the time, and the baby wasn't even scratched. We have bull dozers and plows operating out of Kaibeto and trying to clear the snow away so they can deliver the hay by truck instead of airplanes. The road is blocked up at the Junction now and the mail is three days late. Preacher Bennett tried to take Joe's wife's body in last night but we just got a call from Tuba City saying that he didn't make it. Guess he got stuck and had to sit out in the snow all night with her. One of the bulldozers went that way this morning, so I suppose they have dug him out by this time. We had company of a different sort last night. Two large mountain lions and some of the Navajo are out trying to track them down. Most of the school kids have the mumps so we may have a slump in candy sales for awhile. With love from your mom and me. Dad. PS. Joe Nez just came in and the report about his wife's head being torn off was not true. But I guess it doesn't make much difference since that case of milk definitely finished her off."

Except for a couple personal comments about my school grades, this letter is exactly as my father wrote it all those years ago. Preacher Bennett was from Tuba City and it sounds as if he made it in to Kaibeto to pick up the body but got stuck on the way back. I am puzzled as to why the body had to be taken to Tuba City as the Navajo usually buried their own with their own customs. It may have been a government request because of the way she was killed. Still, it is a puzzle as to why a Presbyterian minister would have been involved. As far as I know, Joe and his family were all traditional Navajos who knew very little about any church.

I love horses. I like their horsey smell. I love the way their coats feel like silk when you run your hands over their backs. I love the way they toss their heads and make soft snorting comments when they see the feed bag coming. I have, however, never been completely at ease when riding on the back of one. Most everyone I knew at Kaibeto seemed to have gone from cradle board to horse back. My mother was a natural born horse woman who made riding look like the simplest of activities. So it always bothered me that I could not sit on a saddle without feeling as if I were three stories off the ground.

When I was in my mid teens I decided that this flaw in my character needed to be corrected. By this time a big government boarding school had been built along Kaibeto Wash across from the trading post. A fellow named John Dodson (more about him later) was employed at the school and he had a couple of horses which he kept in a makeshift corral. John was aware of my shortcomings, and he assured me that his big mare loved to be ridden and was just what I needed to calm my fears. He had even named her "Daisy."

One bright morning Daisy and I proceeded to traverse the area close to the corral. Staying close was more Daisy's idea than mine, as it was evident plodding around

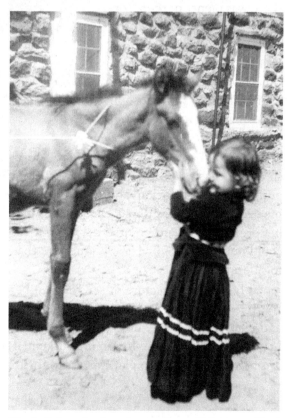

Elizabeth Anne having a face-to-face with her horse friend.

with me on her back was not what she had planned for her morning. We finally were about half a mile up the wash when Daisy, who had never stopped looking longingly back at her horsey home, took off at a pace that would have won the Kentucky Derby. I was enough of a horse woman by this time to handle a full gallop, and I knew that Daisy would stop once she was back at the corral. But horrors! John had taken the other horse out but had left the top post across the gate opening. There was plenty of room for Daisy to get under but absolutely no space for a rider. My only option was to jump and almost without thinking I did. I landed smack on my bosom, knocking the wind out of me and leaving me dazed.

Julia Jones astride an Indian pony.

John had witnessed my graceless performance and lost no time making sure I was basically okay. Then he did the unthinkable. Instead of tenderly putting me in his pickup and taking me home, he very heartlessly hoisted me back up on the traitorous Daisy, said something to her in Navajo, slapped her on the rump and pointed her toward the trading post. The next day I could not get out of bed. I am quite sure that was the last time I ever tried to ride a horse.

I have a great picture of several members of the Winslow Methodist Youth group when they visited later that summer. They are all saddled up and ready to go somewhere with Mother leading the pack. I am standing between Daddy and the Reverend Burkam, not looking one bit sorry that I was being left behind to play hostess to the man of God.

From Highway 89 N there were two ways to get to Kaibeto. The first turn off was about fifteen miles north of Cameron and shook, rattled, and rolled past some dinosaur tracks and piles of something that was thought to be dinosaur poop. There was a small sign with an arrow pointing off to the left which said "dinosaur tracks" but no mention of the poop. I had no idea what those lumps were supposed to be (such things were not discussed in polite society in those days) until as an adult I joined some friends on a proper tour of the area. Having paid quite a sum to see things I had taken for granted as a child and being impressed by our guide, who was quite a nice fellow, I decided to buy into the poop story. After all, there were the tracks, and everyone has to "go" at some time or other.

But I digress and am likely to get us lost. A few more miles and the road skirted Tuba City and then got seriously down to destroying your vehicle and bruising every bone in your body. Accompanied by a football field size plume of dust, twenty miles further came another turn, this one to the north. No sign there, so you had to be a native of Kaibeto to know how to get there.

The other road off HWY 89 took off at the Gap Trading Post. Its only redeeming features were that it cut a good thirty miles off the trip from Cameron and hardly shook your vehicle at all. It began with two clay hills to climb, both of which were wide enough for only one car. If there had been any rain in the past few days, there were always deep gullies cut into both sides of this treacherous trail. Sometimes upon reaching the first hill, it would be obvious your car was not going to fit and so with a swear word or two you trekked all the way back to the Tuba City turn off.

Ever since I have learned to drive, I have always been of the opinion that cars are meant to go forward at all times. Road etiquette required that the descending driver was the one who would back up if another vehicle came along. Never once did I meet another car on either of those hills. This was a very good thing as my skills at driving in reverse are akin to my horsemanship abilities. Once past the hills there were thirty-five miles of shifting sand guaranteed to get you stuck at least once. This was interspersed with rocky outcrops which had to be carefully calculated and eased over. There was also a gated ram pasture which required opening and closing. If I ever saw a ram in there, I have forgotten.

The Gap Road was always more time consuming, but because of the shorter distance, Daddy preferred it. Once he taught me to drive, Daddy drove as little as possible. So, from age fourteen, the minute we were on reservation land he had me get behind the wheel. The Navajo police who knew every one of the few vehicles in the area never stopped us and we never talked about what we would tell them if they did.

The Navajo Reservation completely surrounds the Hopi Reservation. This is not an ideal situation for either tribe, but back when Bob and I were at Rare Metals it didn't seem to be much of an issue. The little church we attended was said to be located half on Hopi land and half on Navajo. I don't think anyone knew this for sure and certainly no one knew which side was which. We were a small and compatible group who enjoyed worshiping and fellowshipping together. It was probably July 4th of 1957 when we had a picnic on Moencopi Wash where some huge cottonwood trees provided luxuriant shade.

I was at the stage of pregnancy where I didn't care if I had a boy or a girl, I just wanted "it" out. I was weary of all the speculation and superstition of "sex telling" that went with pregnancy before the advent of ultrasounds or whatever they call them now. If you carry your baby high, it is a girl, low means a boy. Swing your wedding ring on a string and if it goes from one side to the other it is a boy, if it swings the other way a girl. Rapid heartbeat means boy, not so fast, girl. (Our doctor sort of fancied that one.) I was seated on the ground, leaning against a tree trunk and thinking I was not going to be able to get up until my husband showed up to help.

I dozed off and then heard footsteps. When I opened my eyes, it was not Bob who stood there but a little Hopi man named Mark Quarshero. In his right hand he held a beautifully painted gourd rattle which he began shaking over my bulging middle. It didn't take long for him to tell me there was a little girl in there. He gave me the rattle for her protection, then walked away as if he had done the most normal thing in the world. SueAnne still has the rattle. I still have the sweet memory.

No trading post story today, but we will stay close. The husband of our older daughter just presented me with a lovely bouquet of lilies to thank me for giving birth to his wife. I doubt many sons-in-law take the trouble to thank a mother-in-law for her labor pains. So this is certainly worthy of mention.

Sixty-three years ago, Bob and I were not at the trading post, but did live on the reservation at a place called Rare Metals where he was office manager for a uranium mining company. Tuba city was about ten miles from there on that corduroy gravel road I have described before. After reaching Tuba City, another torturous thirteen miles was required to reach paved Highway 89. We drove a little VW Bug which flitted easily from shake to shock. Being in labor, I felt like its little German engine was sitting on my lap.

Flagstaff was probably a total of seventy-five miles away but seemed more like seventy-five hundred. July 6th was the last day of the All Indian Powwow, so the hospital was filled to overflowing with wounded rodeo cowboy wannabes. I remember seeing beds lined in the hallway. To add to the confusion, half the female residents of Rare Metals were pregnant and had also decided this was a good day to produce an offspring. No husbands allowed in labor or delivery rooms in those days, so Bob had no choice but to join the stereotyped, cigarette smoking, floor pacing group of prospective fathers in the waiting room.

Delivering your baby that day was a bit like playing musical delivery rooms. There were only two such rooms and when one lady seemed to be ready she would be transported. If her labor slowed, then it would become obvious someone else needed the room sooner. Out would come the first, in would go the second until she delivered or was replaced by another fully dilated candidate. Thank God SueAnne showed no reluctance to make her appearance and made her debut on the first trip. A tiny six pounds, twelve ounces, she was plunked down on a metal table where I could see her but not reach her. Her little bird legs were kicking and she screamed as if in terror. It was a hot day, so no one seemed concerned about how badly she was shivering.

Eventually a nurse scooped her up and took her away. Bonding with your baby right after birth was not an option. It was at least two hours before I got to hold her. I am not sure, but I don't think Bob ever got to touch her until the day we were released from the hospital. Tomorrow is her actual birthday, so we will finish this then.

Happy birthday to our oldest who survived being born in the mad house of Flagstaff Hospital during the annual Indian Powwow. As I said yesterday, she was taken away naked and screaming, and it was two hours before I got to hold her long enough to count fingers and toes. My roommate's husband turned out to be a former playmate I enjoyed at Cameron during my parents' visits there when I was a child. He was a peach of a fellow who found a place to dump our overflowing wastebasket and who sneaked in edible food.

Both sets of grandparents showed up for visiting hours, a big endeavor for each couple and a harbinger of the sort of grand parenting which would bless our children.

After all the hubbub died down, I became obsessed with such a desire to have my baby with me, that several times I found myself at the nursery window hoping for just a glimpse. The curtain was always closed, and I was reprimanded and sent back to my room. One afternoon following another unsuccessful foray I noticed that one of the new patients had a small bonfire burning merrily atop her blanket. Wait a minute! Fire! Sleeping patient?? Reverting back to my childhood, I let out one of my famous shrieks the likes of which hadn't been heard since Lollypop ripped open her side. The same nurse who could tote four newborns at once, appeared instantly and yanked the patient out of bed with one hand and folded the burning blanket over with the other. Even while thus occupied she managed to give me a look that left no doubt I was to get along to my own bed.

No mention was ever made of the incident, but the next day the patient did come to thank me. Turns out she had been given something called "Twilight Sleep" while she was having her baby. A smoker, she evidently asked someone for a cigarette soon as she was back in her room. They not only gave it to her but lit it as well. She didn't remember any of this. Bob says he doesn't recall much about getting us out of this bedlam except his pride in now having a little family. I probably rushed him so badly he didn't have time to make any memories. In all fairness to Flagstaff hospital, my mother had surgery there a few months later and received excellent care. Evidently hospitals and Powwows are not a good mix.

Back to the reservation today, but not all the way to Kaibeto. Rare Metals, where Bob and I lived the first years of our marriage is also significant to the Navajo people. The last time I passed by that place, it was surrounded by barbed wire and enormous warnings against trespassing. Yes, it is one of the many locations on the reservation awaiting some sort of deactivation of highly dangerous radioactivity left over from uranium mining. Of course we had no idea of its future when we headed that way with our precious baby. A baby, by the way, who was so jaundiced that by today's medical rules she would have been subjected to about seventeen different tests and never have been allowed to leave the hospital. "Fire fighter nurse" probably would have made sure we were discharged even if SueAnne had turned purple with pink stripes. I related the burning blanket incident to anyone who would listen. Even in those days, such infractions were not conducive to keeping the hard-earned little caps nurses were required to wear.

We stopped at Cameron to introduce SueAnne to her God Parents and someone there told us to make sure she drank lots of water (she hated it) and had a short sunbath every day. The sunbathing advice must have been valid for in a few days the whites of her eyes were no longer the color of egg yolks.

SueAnne may owe her life to the fact that both our mothers were extremely picky about how pristine laundry should appear when hung on a line. "Yellowcake," the sticky yellow cake-mix like stuff that the mining process produced, was everywhere. The men brought home gobs of it on their work clothes. The one washing machine we all shared usually had a good coating left on its bottom. With Mother's admonitions against what she called "tattle tale grey washes" ringing in my ears, I had always rinsed away every last particle before using the machine. Bob had been similarly indoctrinated. Our baby's diapers would have passed the mother test if either of them had happened by. Little did we know that we were rinsing away some very radioactive material. We had been told it was entirely harmless.

After my father had such success teaching me to drive, his next project for me was to pass my skills on down to Mother. Her enthusiasm for this plan was less than nonexistent. She did like our new ride, a huge black Dynaflow equipped Buick Roadmaster which she immediately named "the Hearse". Since I was gone most of the time, common sense dictated a second driver be available should Daddy become ill or injured.

Following Daddy's methodology, we began at the "airport" where mother managed to drive up and down quite well as long as five miles per hour was the prevailing speed. Time to turn onto the road and it soon became obvious that Mother drove wherever she looked. At her rate of locomotion, that didn't create much of a problem. We had progressed only a couple of miles when she decided that she was sure she had left something in the oven and had to get home. She didn't give me a chance to tell her that she needed to find a wider spot for such a maneuver as turning around. With shocking acceleration, she swung the wheel and somehow packed the "Hearse' neatly straight across the high banked dirt road. The big car was so tightly wedged that I had to crawl through the back seat in order to get behind the wheel. No need to tell her that she had forgotten to put the gear shift into P for park as that car wouldn't have gone anywhere.

Those were the days when cars had bumpers that meant business, so with about two inches to spare, I began going backward and forward, knocking down a chunk of embankment with each move and enveloping us in a plume of dust which would have rivaled any dust devil. After five minutes or so, we began to laugh hysterically and regretted the Cokes we had consumed while traipsing around the airport. The big Buick sported neither air conditioning nor power steering, so it was a couple of wilted women who quietly eased it into the back yard where we could hose down the dust and wash out the impacted weeds and pebbles. Daddy never mentioned the couple of big scratches on the front bumper nor did he ever suggest another driving lesson for Mother.

Some of you may have wondered why a place like Kaibeto would have an airport. It really was nothing more than a plowed speck of ground about a mile before the terrain became the little valley called Kaibeto. Why it was created and the occasion which prompted it is not in my memory bank. I am looking at a picture of the one airplane I am sure landed there. Beside the plane stand a couple of dignitaries in double breasted suits looking down benignly on another well-dressed fellow who is kneeling with one arm around me and the other circling the waist of a traditionally dressed little Navajo girl. This would have been about 1939 as we both appear to be about three years old. I am dressed like a proper little white girl.

All eyes are on the adorable little Navajo girl who appears to be unhappy to be in the clutches of a stranger. I am not happy either. That was more than likely because I was being ignored or it could have been because my hair was carefully curled. I would have produced at least three good tantrums before Mother got all that hair arranged in the popular style of Shirley Temple. One half of another fellow, not dressed all that well, must have been the pilot and it is obvious that he was not intended to be in the picture. I feel that this is some sort of a politically staged scene to show the

Group at plane at Kaibito "airport"; Elizabeth Anne in "white girl clothes" and Navajo girl in native dress. – *circa 1939-40*

folks in Washington how well we were treating the Native Americans. It couldn't have been a ploy for their vote as this picture was taken before we so kindly allowed them to go to the polls. So today we are free to imagine whatever we like.

Whatever company scraped out that "airport" did a good job, because as yesterday's tale mentioned, fourteen years later it was still a good place to learn to drive. Several more years down the road, Bob and I found it was a perfect spot for viewing moon, stars, and other heavenly displays.

The Navajo people were usually quiet and soft spoken when they came to the trading post. That changed, however, whenever a group of men got together to gamble. This didn't take place often as it required at least a half dozen participants. If enough wives and daughters congregated in the store with the intent of choosing materials for their next wardrobe addition, the men knew they had plenty of time for a game. Sitting cross legged in a circle shaded by the overhang from the warehouse roof, they would deal out one deck of cards and place another in the center. Each participant would pick up a few cards from the center pile, and the fun began with exchanges from each other and from the remaining pile of cards. Quite suddenly something would match or surface on the discard pile that would cause an eruption of mirth that filled the entire valley. Some of the fellows would be laughing and cheering so hard it caused them to fall backward with legs still crossed like human pretzels. A few coins or dollar bills changed hands and then the whole thing would resume until repeated in just a few minutes. Daddy watched this game many times and never could figure out any rhyme or reason.

The Navajo are not competitive, and without exception every one of these fellows always came away from this raucous sport extremely happy. It is a known fact that men can get pretty giddy when they are spared a shopping excursion with their women folk, but this merriment was beyond even that. Sometimes they would play for a couple of hours and the last wave of mirth was as exuberant as at the beginning. Just one of those things we never quite figured out, but, if we had, it might go a long way to show the world what true sportsmanship should look like.

July 24, 2020. Today's story, although not a happy one, needs to be told.

During WWII daddy corresponded with several of the young Navajo men who had enlisted in the army.

Except for Silas Lefthand, all returned safely, had purification ceremonies (sings) and seemed to go about life as if nothing had happened. The exception was John, who never really seemed to fit in with his fellow tribe members. He found employment at the boarding school the BIA had built during the early fifties and married a local Navajo lady. He and his wife lived in a tiny house on the school grounds rather than a hogan. By the time their first child arrived the friendship between Daddy and John was such that the baby was named after Daddy. So we had "Little Ralph" and "Big Ralph," and Daddy could not have been more proud. John, a gentle soul, who seemed to understand the fears and anxieties suffered by the boarding school children, was a most valued employee. He treated me like a little sister, always teasing me about my inept horseback riding and shaking his head at my attempts to play the flute. Another baby came along and this one, a little girl, was named for my mother.

A Navajo couple outside Kaibeto Trading Post, with "Little Ralph".

All should have been well, but John's experience in the war began taking its toll on him. This gentle, sweet man would turn into a surly, disheartened, and difficult person. After such episodes, John would appear with sincere apologies which Daddy would always accept. If he had kept score of these occurrences, Daddy could have notched the counter clear around. Out of respect, my father never shared the contents of any of the war letters, including John's, but he seemed to understand why John seemed to be collapsing on himself. Even if we had understood about the effects of the terrors witnessed by those in battle, in those long ago days, there would have been no help for John.

After we left the trading post for good, I received a letter telling me that John had succumbed to the effects of his wartime experiences. I never told Daddy.

[Editor's Note: Along with the hard-working and heroic Code Talkers who used the Navajo language to confound the Japanese in the War in the Pacific, there were others who carried the wounds of battle in their bodies, and, as with John, in their souls.]

Mamaw, Ralph's mother, with Elizabeth Anne and "Eddie Girl" a favorite dog, perched at the edge of the bluff that is behind the trading post. At or very near this same spot, Eddie Girl was later bitten by a rattlesnake that was under this or a similar rock. Mamaw was Elizabeth Jones (in this picture, Self) and had earlier been employed at Cameron Trading Post on the Little Colorado River. She and 5 of her 7 children moved as adults from Indiana to Arizona, with two—Elizabeth Anne's father Ralph and her aunt Zada—staying their whole lives. It was at Cameron where Ralph met Julia, who was also working there, and, who became his wife, trader-partner, and Elizabeth Anne's mother. This photo came as a postcard picture taken by Blanche of Kerrville, Texas, postmarked October 17, 1939 using a 1 cent stamp.

July 25, 2020. The screened porch attached to the living quarters at Kaibeto was the only part of the structure which didn't have to be reached by stepping over or under something or watching carefully to keep from breaking an arm or leg. It was obviously an add-on as it was built around one of the outside living room windows. In view of the obstacle course created by the 1934 remodel, the skill in managing to align the porch floor perfectly with the living room floor was nothing short of a miracle. Mother attributed this to the carpentry skills of a Navajo named Gene Gishi. They should have hired him to supervise the entire project.

We loved that porch and in summer months it made each evening a delightfully cool sleeping experience. The cottonwoods whispered softly all night long and the coyotes serenaded the heavens. In the winter, during the short periods I was home, I slept on an extremely uncomfortable sofa which I complained about at every opportunity. One year at Christmas the weather was so mild I threatened to sleep in the big and very comfortable bed on the porch. Mother surprised me by deciding that was a good idea and said she would like to join me. (Daddy snored quite a lot). We made up the bed with flannel sheets and several quilts and, wearing granny gowns and covering our ears with scarves, fell asleep almost instantly.

Come morning I heard Daddy open the door from the living room to the porch, clear his throat and inquire as to when breakfast was going to be ready. Then he continued, "Maybe there won't be any breakfast, considering the predicament you are in?" By this time Mother and I had both realized there was something strange about our pillows. They were wet and we could scarcely turn our heads. It also felt as if our bed clothes weighed a ton. We could tell by the tone of his voice Daddy was enjoying himself immensely, and once we pulled our heads up a bit it was easy to see why. We had slept so soundly that we did not hear the wind which blew at least four inches of snow onto our cozy nest. Our slippers, parked beside the bed, were four blocks of ice. Daddy, doing his best rendition of "He walks with me and He talks with me", enjoyed every minute of shoveling and sweeping us a path and watching us scurry barefooted into the house.

July 26, 2020. Happy Sunday! This seems a good day to explain how the later Kaibeto stories feature two husbands. First, back to the early days. My parents, Ralph Jones and Julia Houck met at Cameron Trading Post. Cameron was a bit of a tourist spot which had the unusual amenities of a small restaurant and hotel. During the early 1930s my grandmother worked there under the grand title of Hotel Hostess. (More on that later.) Enter Julia, the mystery woman, who worked for Mamaw. She would not talk about, nor did we ever find out how she came to be at Cameron. My father came to Cameron to visit his mother (Mamaw) and that makes the end of that part of the story.

What I was told, is that Daddy, a confirmed bachelor of 43, took one look at the lovely Julia and announced she would someday be his wife. Skip ahead to summer of 1955 when I was seated in the coffee shop at Cameron and turned my head to discover next to me was seated the best-looking man I had ever imagined. Bob and I were married in February of 1956. Beginning in July of 1957, three babies followed in rather quick succession. Alas, perhaps we were too young, but eventually, things didn't work out. We were together nearly seventeen years and not long after our divorce I met and married a fellow named Jim. When Jim came into the picture it not only included three teenagers but also a menagerie of animals, a house in constant need of repair and a mother-in-law who was nearing the end of her days. He made it all seem easy.

In the meantime, Bob and I tried to act like a "normal" divorced couple and dislike each other. All those darned kids and their escapades kept getting in the way. We had to be civil to each other when discussing issues such as a daughter getting kicked in the head by a horse or another running off to work in a canning factory or signing for our son's driver's license. We came to realize that our children, created out of our love for each other, were the basis of a unique and lasting friendship. So Bob and I both cherish our many good memories, especially the years at Kaibeto. When I refer to Jim, it is my present husband who somehow fits in the picture and considers Bob's and my children and all their little ones as his too. I can recommend Cameron as a good place to meet a mate!

Postscript. My grandmother later remarried also, and I think her future husband, a man she already knew, probably had to do some of his courting at Cameron.

July 27, 2020. By the time I was seventeen, Daddy had traded in the "Hearse" for another Buick. This one was a gorgeous blue with a white top, its fenders adorned with the four little circles signifying it was another Roadmaster. White leather seats and a dashboard embellished with multiple layers of chrome dazzled my teenage fancy. Unfortunately it used a set of tires about every ten thousand miles. Daddy sent me off to Cameron for a new set of tires, but they did not have them in stock. This suited me just fine as I had made friends with a girl named Eddie who worked in the curio shop and lived in one of the tiny rooms on the second floor of the old hotel. I could bunk in with her for the night which meant we could check out the service station which just happened to be manned by several handsome fellows from Arizona State. Our foray to "check out the candy machine" was highly successful, and we spent a very pleasant evening with our new acquaintances.

Unfortunately, we did not return until nearly midnight. We did not have a key to the hotel and Max, the grumpy old man in charge, was not happy about being up past his bedtime. Next day, same story on the tires. When Max realized I would be spending another night he issued an ultimatum. We were to be in our room by ten or he would lock us out for the night. No problem. The service station had a lovely ladder which would fit right up to our window, and we hid it in the foliage beneath it. The plan worked beautifully, and after cruising Highway 89 long past the witching hour of midnight we gleefully made our ascent and slept like babies.

Babies, indeed, for we forgot about the tell-tell ladder. Eddie didn't lose her job, but I was informed that I was not welcome to spend any more free nights in the hotel. Along with that lecture was the veiled threat that any more of such behavior would mean my parents would be informed of what a "hussy" their daughter had become. The tires arrived and the sweet man from the service station took the car on a trial run all the while lecturing me on the dangers of my behavior. It never occurred to me to back talk any of these adults who had only my best interests at heart. In those days any adult was as authoritative as a parent, and I left grateful that the real authorities at home would never be told about my lack of judgment. Or maybe they were told and realized that I had already had enough punishment to fit the crime. Daddy never sent me off to Cameron on my own again.

July 28, 2020. I keep thinking I will come across an authentic ghost story somewhere along this trading post journey, but no such luck. Not long ago a visiting Arizona historian presented a program at our little village which featured haunted hotels. Zeroing in on the Monte Vista Hotel at Flagstaff, he cited enough hair-raising examples of ghostly occupants to scare away all but the most stout hearted. He did not like it one little bit when I told him of the many nights I had slept there without meeting even one of his ethereal buddies.

From the time I was around ten years old, if a friend from Winslow was headed to Flagstaff at the same time I was due to go back to Kaibeto, I would be dropped off at the hotel. Usually, Daddy was there to meet me, but there were a few times when he couldn't get there until the next morning. The hotel clerk, who knew us, always treated me like a grown up, issuing me one of the big iron keys with the wooden tag, letting me know what time dinner was served, etc. The bellman would carry my suitcase and I would very seriously proffer him a quarter as instructed by my Aunt Zada. Next morning, after an uneventful night's sleep and a good long soak in the claw footed tub, I would feel ever so grown up as I awaited Daddy. My heart always beat a bit faster at the sight of him as he came through the lobby door to escort me to breakfast. Maybe the experience would not have been so delightful if I had known I was surrounded by unearthly beings.

Most trading posts were said to be haunted and ours was no exception. The story of the trader who died of the Spanish flu was factual and I am sure I have written about how his remains were secretly removed lest the Navajos shun the place for fear of his chindi. Evidently, he left complete in body, soul and spirit, as we certainly never had any reason to think any part of him was still lurking, even in the dark cave. I have friends, including a perfectly sensible fellow who lives not far from here, who swear they see the dead and departed regularly, so I suppose such things may exist. There must be something about me they don't like, and I would just as soon it stays that way. But what fun it would have been to write about!

July 29, 2020. Desperate times call for desperate measures. Daddy needed to be gone for medical reasons and Mother couldn't bear not to be with him. It was decided that my Aunt Zada and I would "keep the trading fires burning." In my so selfish almost teen years, this was almost worse news than learning that Daddy was ailing.

Aunt Zada belonged in the world of strict discipline where one changed clothes soon as coming in from school, then tackled homework and piano practice before ever again breathing outside air. Besides that, there was no way this very proper Woman's Club president would understand that Henry Sage's second wife could take thirty minutes to choose the desired color of bias tape. She was sure to loan Hosteen Pish twice as much on his turquoise concho belt as it was worth. How would she know that Mrs. Bennett's old pickup spit gasoline all over you if you filled it with one drop over five gallons? What would she do if someone brought in a half dozen smelly goat skins?

With her love of good manners, she was sure to look everyone straight in the eye and thus insult them. And of course, she would want to call everyone by their given name and thus cause further assault on cultural taboos. Most of this happened, but the Navajos loved Aunt Zada anyhow.

There was something about her eagerness to take care of every need that intrigued them. Not knowing even a half dozen words of Navajo didn't deter her at all. Her attempts at sign language were met with respectful nods and gestures. When someone needed to charge an item, they would point to me to whisper their identity. She would usually repeat it aloud and this always brought gales of laughter. Evidently the name taboo, once transferred, didn't count the second time around. True to her nature, the first few nights after we were in bed, she tried to learn a few basic Navajo words. Also true to her nature, we kept up with every chore in both store and living quarters, so we were extremely weary. Even Aunt Zada's indomitable spirit succumbed to sleep before the coyote pack were halfway through their nightly serenade. It was Daddy's gall bladder and not his heart which was causing his distress.

July 29, 2020. Second post of the day but thought it might bring some of you a smile. While I was writing about Aunt Zada my phone rang at least five times. Someone with an accent wanting to speak to Jim about a Medicare problem. Would not leave a message with me, but when I hung up they called back within minutes using all sorts of threats about losing benefits, etc. if they didn't speak to him in person. By this time I was so immersed in the story that I had a great many Navajo words running around my mind. So I told him off! Not sure if I said that the potatoes were rotten or if the gasoline was full of water, but it worked. No more calls!

July 30, 2020. With Aunt Zada gone and Daddy back at the trading helm, all returned to normal, except--oh dear--no wonderful scent of frying bacon early in the morning. Daddy, diagnosed with a gimpy gall bladder was sentenced to a fat free diet. This presented a tremendous challenge to Mother who, like most cooks of the day, seasoned most every dish from the little grease can sitting on the back of the stove. Every tiny bit of fat had to be sliced off meat. Potatoes and eggs were no longer fried, but boiled. The district supervisor who almost always appeared at dinner time, didn't come around anymore. This robbed Daddy of a companion for listening to his after-dinner ball games. Often a pan, it's bottom scorched and burned from lack of grease, had to be left in the sink to soak overnight.

Aunt Zada Jones Purdy. – *1947*

Oatmeal, still a main stay of breakfast, was not nearly so palatable minus a big chunk of butter. At lunch Vienna sausages gave way to tuna sandwiches. Daddy never insisted that Mother and I should eat only what he did, but it just seemed the right thing to do. Uncreamed canned spinach and peas were more than I could face, and I upped my servings of peanuts and a bottle of Coke to two a day.

One day Daddy announced he never wanted to see another tuna sandwich and with guilty glances toward the store where Mother was taking his place, dispatched his usual can of sausage and stack of crackers in record time. I kept his secret, only making sure that the next day I had my own supply of Vienna delicacies. A couple of days later we were expecting company and Mother needed to make a big pot of her famous pinto beans. This required at least a cup of bacon grease. So bacon had to be fried and Mother said it would be a sin to waste it. Pies to be baked--more bacon grease if the crusts were to be decent. Meanwhile, Daddy didn't seem to be any worse for all his cheating, and he was certainly a lot more cheerful. Mr. Ellison began showing up at dinner hour again which meant Mother could get to bed before Daddy began snoring. Maybe the diagnosis was wrong or maybe Daddy's gall bladder decided that processing the contents of that little grease can wasn't so terrible after all. It was nice to get back to normal.

July 31, 2020. One of my readers commented on how a fifty-pound flour sack provided enough material for a dress for her when she was a child. Once I was five, there were no flour sacks made large enough to make any sort of outfit for me. That was probably a good thing as Mother's many talents did not include dress making. In those long ago days, every woman worthy of her "homemaker" title felt duty bound to turn those pretty flour sacks into something useful, so Mother did make a collection of aprons. I call them a collection because no two were alike and none of them were smoothly gathered or evenly hemmed. With no electricity, Mother had to use a treadle machine and I soon learned that being in the store with Daddy, no matter what sort of assignment he might give, was preferable to being around Mother when the sewing urge struck.

In Junior High, we had to take Home Economics (not my favorite class) and part of the torture of sewing class was mastering a treadle machine. I soon learned why Mother turned into "Brunhilda the Witch" when she sewed. How anyone could hold fabric in place while guiding it under that silly little foot thing and at the same time peddle back and forth with both feet, was impossible. These were also the times when we "belaganas" [Navajo term for "white people" derived from how they heard the Spanish word "Americanas." Eds.] tended to think we were smarter than Native Americans. During that sewing class I realized that there was not a white person on the face of the earth who could sew like the average Navajo lady.

We sold many yards of luscious velvet which I couldn't even cut straight. Most of the ladies either grabbed the scissors from me and performed the operation before I could ruin their purchase or made a small slash and then tore it unerringly straight right off the bolt. Thanks to the Singer Company, who sent salesmen around every year or so, they did have treadle machines, but never a pattern. Decorated with silver buttons, or just plain, those velvet blouses were always perfection and each one fit perfectly. Skirts made from various other fabrics, always hung evenly and were bound along the bottom with bias tape which was perfectly stitched in place. This talent seemed to be the blessing of every Navajo lady, as I never saw one woman who was not attired as if she had been fitted by the Queen's dressmaker.

August 1, 2020. I mentioned silver buttons yesterday when writing about the skills of every Navajo seamstress. We didn't sell such things, so I am not sure where they came from. Maybe they were Zuni made like so much of the early Navajo jewelry. I do know one main source and that was the US Government. In fact almost every silver button I saw during my childhood was a product of our good old Uncle Sam. Dimes and quarters with a thin copper wire welded onto their "tail" side were attached decoratively to the front of nearly every velvet blouse. This, of course, defaced the coins and made them worthless for spending. Whoever did the welding always seemed to do the job extremely well and no amount of filing would completely remove the lump left by the copper. I think Daddy realized how much time it took to try to remove the evidence and so didn't quibble about accepting them.

By the time Bob and I took over the trading post the coin button was no longer so popular so there was quite a collection of mutilated quarters and dimes rattling around in the back of the cash register drawer. Yes, by this time we had a real cash register which was a first cousin to the scales we used for weighing potatoes, and both looked exactly like the ones used by the Olsons from Little House on the Prairie. Using this register required pulling a handle which opened the drawer so slowly that even our most dedicated devotees of Navajo time would begin to show signs of impatience. Hoping to lighten the load and thus speed the process a bit, we removed all the soldered coinage and tried including a few in wrapped coins we sent to the bank. Our deposits came back minus those tiny amounts.

Once on our way home from a vacation we passed through Las Vegas and thought to try our luck at one of the casinos. We just happened to have a few of these lumpy coins with us and decided to see if they might work. No problem! The machines were perfectly willing to give us back real dimes and quarters when they gave back anything at all, which was seldom. Then we began hearing calls for machine repair and it was always for one of the machines we had been playing. Uneasy about being in a casino in the first place, we beat a fast retreat, never to return. I have no idea what happened to those coins. I wish I had saved a few just for the memories.

August 3, 2020. The year I started 5th grade Aunt Zada went off to the University of Arizona to get her Masters. A young couple named Don and Theresa rented the house. Being the challenge I was, it could have been they were paid to stay there. I have racked my brain trying to remember what we did with Uncle John that year, as at that time 606 West Oak had only two bedrooms. Surely he didn't bunk in the caboose of the Super Chief all that time [**Editor's Note:** John was a railroad conductor.].

Come spring, Don got a better job offer so there was no one to look after me. I was delighted because I did not care for my teacher that year. She was one of those teachers who made sure every student was on the same page at the same time. At her command of "pencils up" we were required to hold those freshly sharpened number 2 leads where she could see them and were not allowed to apply them to paper until we heard "pencils down." She then walked the aisles, making sure that every last one of us had every line written to perfection.

My friend John and I were always among the first to complete the assignment and spent the rest of the time sneaking notes about our dreams of escaping. He always wanted to slide down the fire escape. I wanted to go back to the reservation. One afternoon during health class our teacher became very serious as she explained the necessity of washing our "privates" each day. I didn't know I had any privates that needed washing, and on the way home from school when I asked John if he had any, he replied that the only privates he ever heard of were in the army. As far as he knew they had all come back home or had been promoted to generals or something. If only our teacher had used the term "spit bath" I would have understood that she was talking about the ritual with the granite basin, washcloth and Lux soap to which Mother had introduced me using a much more easily understood and graphic vocabulary.

By this time I had been told that I would have to return to the trading post and was delightedly anticipating several months of Mother's lackadaisical approach to home schooling. So I was completely shocked when on my last Friday under this teacher's tutelage, she called me to the front of the room, put her arms around me and tearfully announced my departure. Then she added that I would be transferring to the Tuba City School system. It still takes me awhile to get over the shock of that announcement. Continued tomorrow.

August 6, 2020. I never did figure out which one of my treacherous parents decided to comply with the law and make sure my rebellious little behind was in a classroom for the remainder of my fifth-grade year. A week after my departure from my former class, I found myself being boarded with the Presbyterian minister's family in Tuba City. The pastor and his wife were kind and loving just as you would expect of folks in that position. Unfortunately, they had two sons slightly younger than I, who were being raised with some sort of no discipline philosophy. I am sure one of them had to give up his bedroom to accommodate me, but both of them disliked me intensely. There had been only one other girl in our Winslow neighborhood, and she and I played with a large group of boys, who seemed to think we were just part of the gang. So it was hard for me to realize these two rather cute little males were responsible for slimy critters in my bed and sand in my shoes.

School was not much better than before. It was a two-room arrangement consisting of all eight grades and I can't remember if I was the only fifth grader or if my former teacher had taught us so thoroughly that I was ahead of the materials presented. I don't recall a single time of being personally instructed from any of the textbooks. No homework was ever assigned. I pretty much sat idly and listened to the other grades. Then came Friday afternoon and following recess the world grew bright again. The students from the other room squeezed in with us and their teacher passed out tattered and dog-eared song books. The ancient upright piano in our room came to life as she led us in everything from "Come with Me Lucille, in my Merry Oldsmobile" to "The Old Rugged Cross" and the "Marine's Hymn."

As if that were not enough joy, soon as I exited the classroom on Friday, the little red Buick would be waiting. Daddy would have already picked up my suitcase and off we would go, bumpety bump down the terrible washboard road toward Kaibeto. I have no report cards or any sort of record from that school to show I was promoted. Maybe my Winslow teacher had put in a good word for me for I was admitted to sixth grade in Wilson School in Winslow without incident. Of course she never dreamed that her lesson about "privates" went completely over my head.

August 6, 2020. I got some very good responses to my second-grade story of a Japanese "prison" camp at Leupp. There was such a place, but it was called an internment camp and according to one account was manned by Military Police. The two articles about it I have read so far do not agree in several points. So here is a second-grade version to add to the mix.

Calling the camp a prison camp gave folks the idea that it was filled with Japanese prisoners of war. According to both articles, the inmate population was made up of Japanese US citizens who were incensed at being uprooted and treated as the enemy. They did not submit peacefully, were known as troublemakers and thus ended up at Leupp. Aunt Zada was one of two teachers at the Leupp school, and since I was living with her in Winslow for the school year, I went with her to Leupp.

The Military Police term puzzles me as I have memories of Zada and me taking our meals at the "mess hall" with older gentlemen in impressive uniforms. It was a big room and a very long table with every seat taken, so quite a presence for supervising the fifty to eighty prisoners mentioned in both accounts I read. I also have distinct and frightening memories of row upon row of soldiers, marching in formation, all of them wearing gas masks.

During the week, Zada and I boarded with Miss Pike, a missionary lady, who lived in Old Leupp. Her house was within walking distance of the mess hall and school. The other teacher, Mrs. Zimmerman, drove back and forth to Winslow each day and we came with her on Monday morning and left with her on Friday. Zada and I had a "house boy" from the camp. His name was Yama, and he arrived every morning while we were still in bed and built a fire, made tea and treated us with great respect. Zada being Zada, those two soon became seriously busy early in the day.

Tomorrow I will share some of my memories of how Zada and I fared that year. Then you can all "Google up a storm" and prove me right or wrong.

August 7, 2020. After the army, which was not really an army, and the prisoners, who were not really prisoners, mysteriously disappeared from Leupp there were too few students to justify employing two teachers. Zada, a non-driver, chose to stay. Uncle John's railroad job would have prevented him from driving us, and I can't remember how we commuted. What I do remember, oh, how well I remember, was the curriculum I had to endure.

Because the sprinkling of students who remained spanned at least six or seven grades, poor Zada became like that earthy saying of the day--a chicken with its head chopped off. She never sat behind her desk but moved constantly from student to student--sixth grade geography--fifth grade English--third grade spelling and on and on. It all had to be accomplished for each student every single day.

Then there was the lone second grader who received no attention at all until school was over and we were walking to Miss Pike's house. That is when I was given a spelling review which meant I had to not only spell the word but say what it meant and use it in a sentence. Then I was grilled on addition and subtraction facts. This usually got us in the front door and into our room where she had stashed a complete set of second grade textbooks. While Zada prepared our dinner, I was given a reading assignment and dessert always included around forty questions about what I had read. In my rebellious mind I had been sentenced to a twenty-four-hour school, and had Zada been like my mother, my mouth would have been super clean and smelling like Life Boy soap a great deal of the time. She never once lost patience with me even when I threw a fit when she assigned me my own section of blackboard and found time every morning to cover it with math problems.

The last couple months of that year, Miss Pike disappeared too. Maybe she was the "Miss Marple" of the Leupp set up--who knows? We finished the year at Leupp Trading Post with Ida Mae Borum and her daughter Tinky. I think after she became a widow Ida Mae ran the trading post all by herself. Unlike Kaibeto, the living quarters at Leupp were cozy and beautiful. Best of all, Tink, who was a few grades ahead of me, loved to help me with the hated cursive writing and reading comprehension. After dinner there was some blessed free time for play. We did get into a lot of trouble, but now I can't remember what we did that was so bad. I think it had something to do with the fact that both Zada and Ida Mae thought they were supposed to be raising young ladies. As for me, school is still out on that one.

August 8, 2020. Chopping some celery a few minutes ago when the name "Tillman Hadley" popped into my mind. For weeks I have been searching my memory bank for that name. This is one of those stories I didn't witness, but which has been told so many times I am quite sure of its authenticity. It was also printed in a true detective magazine which my mother proudly showed to every visitor. Much to Mother's disgust, the magazine disappeared. She always said she knew who filched it, but she didn't have sufficient proof to confront the culprit. That may have been a good thing as by now we all know what Mother was capable of if she smelled a rat!

According to the magazine, Tillman Hadley, if my memory is correct, was one of the first Navajo policemen and was quite well known for his crime solving abilities. That doesn't mean there was a whole lot of crime on the Rez in the 1940s. We can surmise that his "precinct", which was probably the entire western part of the Rez, was so large that there were bound to be a few cases to solve every now and again.

I have already written about the road between Kaibeto and Tonalea which was an unpaved nightmare under the best of conditions and nigh on impossible for travel more often than not. One spot on that grueling trail was called "The Divide" and was given that name because it was the highest spot in elevation between the two trading posts. It also might have been so titled because it was a likely location for one's soul and body to be severed and thus divided forever. The divide hill was a total blind spot with trees on both sides so no place to pull over if another vehicle was approaching. A pullover spot would have been useless for the road surface was so rocky that the usual tell all plume of dust did not generate. There was no way to know if a head on collision was imminent.

Our sturdy little Buick was able to creep slowly up that hill, but most of the ancient conveyances of that time had to get a running start to clear the big hump on top. With engine revving and driver either praying or swearing, everyone was so relieved to have avoided disaster that it is doubtful that anybody ever noticed the tiny ravine off to the left about forty feet on the Kaibeto side. And down that ravine...... This is a murder mystery and you have now completed chapter one.

August 9, 2020. Meanwhile back at the trading post, Daddy was having a hard time understanding the very elderly Hosteen Bigman who was gesturing wildly and using all sorts of Navajo vocabulary which had nothing to do with our usual fare of axle grease, pawn, and the price of potatoes. He finally discerned that something or someone was dead and that someone was probably a white man. Mr. Bigman was not certain enough of that fact to take a close look and needed a second opinion.

Summoning Mother to mind the store, Daddy stuffed a very reluctant Hosteen Bigman into the passenger seat of the Buick and started following his increasingly hesitant gestures toward the road to Tonalea. Just before reaching the summit of the Divide, Hosteen became extremely agitated, pushing himself excitedly up and down on the car seat and pointing toward a tiny ravine. Figuring that the old man needed to relieve himself, Daddy stopped the car and was surprised when after exiting the car, Hosteen desperately signaled that Daddy was to follow. It took only few steps for Daddy to understand his actions. Not quite visible from the road with his head terribly smashed was the body of an old gold prospector who always stayed underneath tribal radar and had never made friends with anyone. I can't recall if his mule was patiently standing by, but I do remember clearly that his expensive boots were missing. Nothing for Daddy to do but drive back to Kaibeto, keeping his fingers crossed that the telephone was working and notify the famous tribal policeman Tillman Hadley that he had a crime to solve.

August 10, 2020. If a serious crime like murder occurs on the Rez, the FBI has jurisdiction. At least that was the procedure when the murdered body of the old prospector made its appearance. I think it might be the same today, but am not sure.

I always thought this arrangement was somewhat of an insult to tribal officers, who would have been much more knowledgeable about what conditions might bring on something so terrible. It was also demoralizing for the FBI agents who did not speak a word of Navajo and hadn't an inkling of the culture. To the best of my memory, from reading the True Detective account, even though Daddy called the Police at Tuba City, the FBI arrived before the esteemed officer Hadley. And here, dear readers, is when a pin gets stuck in that wonderful balloon of suspense we have been building. As the FBI agents stood about scratching their heads and wondering how to begin a hogan-to-hogan canvas in their search for likely suspects, Tillmann Hadley worked his way down into the little ravine. Surveying the scene for less than a minute, he immediately eliminated about thirty thousand suspects by announcing that no Navajo would have done this. "This man's boots are missing", he pointed out. "No Navajo will ever take anything from a dead body, so we need to look for someone who is not from around here."

It didn't take Officer Hadley but a couple days, with the help of the "moccasin telegraph", to find a fellow from another tribe who was wearing a pair of ill-fitting boots. He confessed not only to the killing and boot theft but also had taken the prospector's money which was a little over fifty cents. I can't recall the name of the tribe or what the killer was doing in Navajo country. What is etched in my memory is how every time we passed that spot by the ravine, Daddy would slow the car down to a crawl, roll down the window and pointing dramatically would announce, "That's the spot, right down there, where we found that poor old man who had been murdered." He never offered to stop and give me a closer look and that was okay. I really didn't believe in the Chindi but was just as glad not to take any chances.

August 11, 2020. In the summer of 1956, Bob and I were still very much newlyweds and enjoyed getting away to ourselves as often as we could afford to. Our favorite trip was the short, jolting jaunt to Kaibeto where we were sure to receive not only the affection of my parents but a huge "care package" to bolster our slim finances. No refrigeration in our little VW Beetle, so the rising elevation made the trip more enjoyable with each mile.

June 30th of that year we arrived to find Mother looking rather exasperated and puzzled. She asked us if we had seen anything resembling an airliner stranded along our route. Then she explained that she had just had a call from TWA wanting to know if anyone in our area had reported finding a downed aircraft. She had replied that if such a thing had happened anywhere within a hundred square miles, she would have heard about it within a very short time. Her next comment was to wonder how anyone could lose anything as large as a commercial airplane. It had probably already landed in Salt Lake City or Denver or wherever it was supposed to land, and the pilot forgot to let anyone know they had arrived.

We enjoyed our evening together and forgot all about the puzzling call. Our cute little Bug also lacked a radio, so it wasn't until the next day that we learned that United Airlines was also missing an aircraft and that the two had a tragic meeting over Grand Canyon. All 128 people aboard the two planes lost their lives, the greatest commercial airline disaster at that point in our country's history. Not a pretty tale, but very much a part of our Northern Arizona History.

Once upon a time Daddy had persuaded Mother to enjoy a flight in a glass bottomed seaplane. I don't think she had ever quite forgiven him, and I know she never boarded another airplane.

August 12, 2020. June bugs and bats! Kaibeto had a plethora of both. After a long day in the trading post Mother used to love to swing in the hammock Daddy had suspended between a couple of the big cottonwoods in the front yard. Mother was the only person I ever knew who could sit in a hammock with her legs crossed beneath herself and sway back and forth for hours at a time. Daddy had also fashioned a swing for me, the old-fashioned kind with ropes tied to the limb of a tree and a board for a seat.

I loved to join Mother on those evenings but there were two entities which kept my nerves jingling and my heart pounding. The first were the blasted June bugs. They probably had another more technical name, but that was what Mother called them. They originated in the form of what Daddy called grub worms and were prized by him for fishing bait. The day before a fishing trip, we could dig them up around the roots of the cottonwoods. I didn't mind them in that form for they stayed put in our container of choice. The ones who escaped our digging forays turned themselves into ugly, buzzing little missiles who worked themselves up out of the rock-hard ground and then flew blindly straight toward the sky. After enjoying about eight seconds of life they became dinner for one of the dozens of bats which came soaring under the trees in search of such delicacies. The bats fascinated me, but the June bugs terrified me. I was sure one would eventually tangle its sticky little legs in my hair.

Mother wasn't impressed by either. No June bug ever emerged from the ground directly under her hammock, but beneath my swing seemed to be their favorite entrance into civilization. No bat ever dared to come within inches of her face to catch dinner. They practically brushed my nose as they streaked after their prey. How those bats could tell the difference between my shrieking and the droning from the bug and unerringly pick up his meal is still a mystery to me.

We never figured out where the bats hung out during the day. They showed up every year until the bug buffet was exhausted. Even though it was still summer, our winged companions would disappear until the first ugly little head popped up the following year. When I was teaching it was a joy to educate children about the value and wonder of bats and watch their faces change from distaste to enlightenment. As for the June bugs--I would still run shrieking and arms flailing if I saw one.

August 14, 2020. Several years ago, my younger daughter posted a picture of my three-year-old father along with his baby brother and older sister. It popped up again today and reminded me of the time when that older

Elizabeth Anne, an only child, had many doll playmates and posed them here beside her trading post home.

sister died, and Daddy had to go all the way to San Gabriel in California for her funeral. I was devastated by my aunt's death. She had never been able to have children and so had practically adopted me and my seven cousins. I think I was about eleven and had only been to one funeral because children were mostly excluded from such rites in those days. The grimness and grief of that occasion had made me resolve never to attend another. Daddy gave me the choice of going or staying to help Mother and I chose to stay.

It was a busy season when wool buying was finished and lamb season hadn't begun. Ceremonial dances and curing sings were stirring up the population's need for supplies to share as they visited one camp and then another. Our helper Jack Hudson's family was involved in some of this so Mother and I were mostly on our own. I think that even she ate a few cans of the life sustaining Vienna sausages during that time. I know she did the peanuts and Coke thing a time or two.

After what seemed like a month (it was probably more like six days) Daddy returned to a sticky bull pen floor, an overflowing bottle cap catcher, a collection of watermelon rinds out front and two exhausted females. There may have even been a few dirty dishes in the sink although I can't imagine Mother actually letting things get that far out of whack. We had never dreamed that our slow-moving genial head of household accomplished so much in the course of each day. By the next morning he had everything put to rights, and I think he was a bit pleased that he had come home to find us a bit discombobulated. The ledger book and pawn records were in good order and testified to the extraordinary volume of business we had handled. When Mother found time to do that was a puzzle, and I know that after Lollypop and I found our way to bed she probably burned several midnight lamps of kerosene oil. They were a good team.

October 3, 2020. I have been blessed by more than a few comments about no more Kaibeto stories. Truth be told, Kaibeto, rather like Brigadoon, sort of disappeared into the mists of time. I ran out of memories. Oh, there were bits and pieces, but nothing that would make up a tale worth telling. Then I remembered Mr. Heiser. Mr. Heiser was one of the salesmen who traveled the reservation with the hope of supplying traders with some of the goods which were a bit out of the ordinary and not stocked by Babbit Brothers or Associated Grocers. He was a rotund, jolly fellow and if I remember correctly, was responsible for our rather impressive display of leather goods, bridles, and saddles and such.

When Mr. Heiser arrived, Daddy always had to find a chair and seat him behind the counter because his size prevented him from standing for more than a few minutes. No matter where Daddy placed the chair, Mr. Heiser always repositioned it so that it was within arm's reach of the bin which held the colorful and very sweet old-fashioned candies. There was no such thing as wrapped penny candy in those days, and it was impossible to pass that bin and not sample its wares. The flies also loved it! Then I was hoisted up onto his big, soft lap which provided him an excuse to try to figure out just which succulent piece was the best. I had my favorites and so did he. I also usually had a tummy ache by the time Mr. Heiser departed.

Every Christmas I received a doll from Mr. Heiser--not just ordinary dolls, but gorgeous, beautifully appointed collector's examples--Scarlet O'Hara, Sonja Henie (the skater) and even Shirley Temple. I was not allowed to play with these dolls, and I think Mother treasured them far more than I ever did. She brought them out each Christmas where they were displayed behind the tree nestled in sparkly rolls of white cotton. It was not until my parents retired that she finally consented to giving me the dolls. I could scarcely wait to give them to my girls, but my joy was short lived. They came out of their boxes in pieces, their eyes disappeared into their beautifully made-up fragile faces and their costumes were faded and limp. Probably because of the war effort, these precious babies had been held together with some sort of cheap elastic which had disintegrated between the time of my childhood and that of my own girls. So, I was left with nothing but memories of a dear old man who took time to show love to a little girl who was not a grandchild, but certainly treated like one. Not a bad trade at all!

ELIZABETH ANNE JONES DEWVEALL

AUTHOR ELIZABETH ANNE DEWVEALL JONES has been playing the flute since her days when growing up on the Navajo Indian Reservation at the Kaibeto Trading Post. A lifelong Arizonan with an interest in the state's past, she also became a source for history of the Kaibito region for the period since 1936, when she was born to trader parents. Childhood activities and observations on the reservation –watching Natives and Anglos interact with and among themselves and with their land and livelihoods, witnessing extremes of weather, exploring the desert landscape, learning some Navajo words and about Native customs as well as her own, herself trading as a young merchant, and imagining—all this was the early learning foundation for Elizabeth Anne's life. Formal schooling both on and off the reservation and at times at home in the trading post were added, some of it in Leupp and much of it in Winslow where she lived with her Aunt Zada's and Uncle John's family during the academic year, going home to the trading post for holidays and summer vacations. From Winslow High School she went on with her education at Arizona State University and Northern Arizona State University where she took courses in the flute and journalism. Married, she went back with her husband to manage the trading post where she grew up. Remarried, she lived for a time in Leupp, where many years before she had gone to school with her Aunt Zada as her teacher. She has provided memories and historical photographs to the Old Trail Museum of Winslow and contributed letters to Arizona Highways. Elizabeth Anne now lives in Mesa, Arizona, surrounded by friends and family members including three children, five granddaughters and twelve great grandchildren.

ACKNOWLEDGMENTS

In putting this book together, the editors are grateful for help and encouragement from many family members, and we make special mention of the following: Pete Langford who saw these writings on Facebook and with Katherine Lopez copied them off and saved them; Robin Varnum for preserving family pictures of little Elizabeth Anne in a Navajo dress, of Trader Ralph at the road sign, of Zada, and of Julia on a horse as well as Juris Zagarins for tweaking these photos for publication; Katie Langford for journalistic advice; Richard and Teddy Jones for searching out old maps of the Kaibito area; Arizona Memory Project; Arizona Library; Arizona Office of Tourism and U.S. Geological Survey for use of Kaibito maps; Jerome Greene, retired National Park Service historian for advice; Old Trails Museum of Winslow, Arizona; Heard Museum; Northern Arizona University; Gladwell Richardson for his Kaibito entries in his book Navajo Trader and for his family's pioneering development and operation of their several trading posts in the region; and, of course, Elizabeth Anne herself for Kaibeto Trading Post pictures and for turning her talented writer's hand to the task of setting down her well-recalled memories for us.

We editors have as our main qualifications having experienced the Kaibeto Trading Post as boys when Anne was growing up and keeping "in the loop" with our cousin who lived there while also receiving family letters telling of the family's daily lives about what seemed to us adventures. The Reverend Bob Jones is a minister living in California at Guerneville on the Russian River who has written varied books on religion and reports of the lives of those in his home town and in Scranton, Pennsylvania as well as a long stint writing a newspaper column. Bill Jones worked as a geologist and for the National Park Service as a ranger and naturalist and park planner with assignments that included Canyon de Chelly and Chaco Canyon parks on the Navajo Reservation and has also been an editor and a published author of magazine articles and books.

SUGGESTED READINGS

- *Along Navajo Trails: recollections of a trader,*
  by Will Evans; Utah State University Press, 2005.

- *Both Sides of the Bull Pen: Navajo trade and posts,*
  by Robert McPherson; University of Oklahoma Press, 2017.

- *Dine'ji' Na'nitin: Navajo Traditional Teachings and History,*
  by Robert S. McPherson; University Press of Colorado, 2012.

- *Hubbell Trading Post: Trade, Tourism, and the Navajo Southwest,*
  by Erica Cottam; University of Oklahoma Press, 2015.

- *In Red Man's Land: a study of the American Indian,*
  by Francis E. Leupp; Fleming H. Revell, 1914.
  Reprinted by Rio Grande Press, 1976.

- *The Mountain Chant: a Navajo ceremony,*
  by Washington Matthews; University of Utah Press, 1997.

- *The Night Chant: a Navajo ceremony,*
  by Washington Matthews; University of Utah Press, 1995.

- *Navajoland: a Native son shares his legacy,*
  by LeRoy DeJolie; Arizona Highways Special Scenic Collection, 2005.

- *Navajo Places: history, legend, landscape,*
  by Lawrence D. Linford; University of Utah Press, 2000.

- *Navaho Legends,*
  by Washington Matthews; University of Utah Press, 2004.

- *Navajo Trader,*
  by Gladwell Richardson; University of Utah Press, 1986.

- *Navajo Tradition, Mormon Life,*
  by Robert S. McPherson, Jim Dandy, Sarah E. Burak; University of Utah Press, 2012.

- *Sacred Land, Sacred View: Navajo perceptions of the Four Corners region,*
  by Robert S. McPherson; University Press of Colorado, 1992.

Rattle used by a Hopi man over Elizabeth Anne's bulging middle to correctly predict a daughter-to-be (SueAnne) was in there. From the collection of SueAnne Suffolk. *See story on page 86.*

INDEX

Made in the USA
Middletown, DE
10 April 2023

28461981R00070